FAMILIES
WHERE GRACE
IS IN PLACE

Jeff VanVonderen

BETHANYHOUSE

a division of Baker Publishing Group
Minneapolis, Minnesota

© 1992, 2010 by Jeff VanVonderen

Published by Bethany House Publishers
11400 Hampshire Avenue South
Bloomington, Minnesota 55438
www.bethanyhouse.com

Bethany House Publishers is a division of
Baker Publishing Group, Grand Rapids, Michigan.

Printed in the United States of America

Library of Congress Cataloging-in-Publication Data
VanVonderen, Jeffrey.
    Families where grace is in place : building a home free of manipulation, legalism, and shame / Jeff VanVonderen.
        p.   cm.
    Summary: "Drawing on both his professional counseling and personal experience, the author shows readers how to nurture God-honoring family relationships free of manipulation, legalism, and shame. The new [second] edition includes discussion questions for groups and for individuals or couples"—Provided by publisher.
    ISBN 978-0-7642-0793-8 (pbk. : alk. paper)
    1. Family—Religious life. 2. Christian life. I. Title.
BV4526.3.V36   2010
248.8'45—dc22   2010016357

Study questions at the end of each chapter have been added to the original version of the book for use in families or small groups.

Unless otherwise indentified, scripture quotations are from the New American Standard Bible®, copyright © 1960, 1962, 1963, 1968, 1971, 1972, 1973, 1975, 1977, 1995 by The Lockman Foundation. Used by permission.

Scripture quotations identified NIV are from the Holy Bible, New International Version®. NIV®. Copyright © 1973, 1978, 1984 by Biblica, Inc.™ Used by permission of Zondervan. All rights reserved worldwide. www.zondervan.com

Verses marked AMP are from the Amplified® Bible, copyright © 1954, 1958, 1962, 1964, 1965, 1987 by The Lockman Foundation. Used by permission.

Scripture quotations identified TLB are from The Living Bible, copyright © 1971. Used by permission of Tyndale House Publishers, Inc., Wheaton, Illinois 60189. All rights reserved.

Cover design by Eric Walljasper

18 19 20 21 22 23 24   13 12 11 10 9 8 7

JEFF VANVONDEREN is an internationally known speaker on addictions and church and family wellness. He has worked as a counselor in both residential and outpatient treatment settings as well as in the religious community, taught at the college and university level, and is the author of several books, including *Tired of Trying to Measure Up*, *The Subtle Power of Spiritual Abuse*, and *Good News for the Chemically Dependent and Those Who Love Them*. Jeff is one of the featured interventionists on A&E network's Emmy Award-winning documentary series *Intervention*, which has won four Prism Awards. He has also appeared on *Oprah*, the *Today* show, and *Larry King Live*. He has nine grandchildren and makes his home in Wisconsin.

Contents

PART I

Families Where Grace Is Not in Place

Introduction

A man asked his twelve-year-old daughter one day, "Chrissy, can you do something for me?"

"Sure, Dad," Chrissy answered. "What would you like me to do?"

"Right now I need to run an errand. But later on I have to do some work on that fence over there," he said, pointing to the high old fence that stood at the back of their property. "Would you please clean up the debris that's all along the edge of it? You can put it in these bags, and when I get back I'll carry them away."

"Okay, Dad," she replied.

The dad left, and Chrissy started on her task. In less than an hour she was finished with the entire job. Her dad wasn't home yet, so she tried to think of something else to do to help. Looking at the old fence, she thought, *I'll bet dad is going to paint this old fence. I'll give him a head start. He'll sure be surprised when he gets home.*

The sun was hot, the brush was stiff, and the fence was high. After about an hour Chrissy was tired, sweaty, and discouraged. She looked at what she'd accomplished so far. *What a bogus job. I give up. I'm a terrible helper.*

Just then Chrissy's dad pulled up. But he didn't get out of the car. He just sat there looking at the fence. The streaky brush marks spoke of an old paintbrush in inexperienced hands. He could picture his sweet daughter perched on tiptoe, working hard.

When he got out of the car there was Chrissy. She was covered with so much dirt and paint that it was hard to see her skin. As he got a closer look, he could see the trails of sweat and tears through the grime on her face.

Chrissy ran to him. "Daddy, I wanted to help so much," she cried.

Chrissy's dad led her to a nearby lawn chair. Sitting down with her on his lap he said, "Sweetie, I've got some bad news, some *worse* news, and some good news.

"The bad news is that I have new brushes and a step stool in the trunk of my car. I ran the errand to pick up those things at the hardware store. That brush you were using belonged to your grandpa. It isn't useful for much more than a keepsake."

"Well, that's the bad news," said Chrissy. "What's the worse news?"

"The worse news is that I'm going to tear down the fence."

"What? After all that work! Why?"

"Because it's served its purpose, it can't be repaired, and I have the stuff right over there by the garage to build a brand-new one. Ready for the good news?" Dad asked anxiously.

"I suppose." Chrissy sniffed.

Chrissy's dad took her face in his hands, looked full into her eyes and, with tears in his own, said, "Chrissy, I really love you. And I am so proud that you gave that old fence a try. Why don't you get in the car and I'll take you out for some ice cream."

"After I wasted all that time and made a terrible mess?"

"Well, you know," her father countered, "with the lousy tools you had you didn't stand a very good chance. And besides that, it wasn't even your job. So let's have some ice cream. After that, if you're still game, we can build the new fence together. This one will be much prettier. And it's specially designed to let the sun shine in and let the breeze blow through our yard. . . ."

The story of Chrissy and her dad is very much like that of so many Christian parents who come to me for pastoral advice and family counseling. They want to do the right thing. They try like crazy to have a Christian marriage and to raise Christian kids. But they've ended up tired, discouraged, and feeling like failures.

If you have ever felt this way, I have news for you. Few of us are equipped to do the *right job* when it comes to creating the best relationship with our spouse, or when it comes to training and guiding our children. Like Chrissy, we see that there is a big job to be done, and we try to use the best relationship tools we know—but in the end, we too often wind up feeling as if we've done a terrible job. We don't stop to think that maybe our tools are inadequate for the job. No wonder we feel tired and discouraged! For some, it will be a little frightening to think, *Maybe I've gone to all those seminars and heard all those tapes on how to take charge of my family relationships, and the techniques and principles they offer don't do the job.*

There are many books available on the behaviors and attitudes that characterize a Christian family: how to have a Christian marriage; how to make your kids clean their room; how to get your sex life back; how to get your spouse to respond the way you want him/her to, and a host of other formula-oriented books. There are also many books that present ways to transfer Christian values to members of the family. And there are still others that talk about how to build positive self-esteem in family members.

Too often, though, the work we try to do as Christian spouses and parents is not the right job at all. We focus on "unspiritual" or wrong behavior, then we set out to apply pressure, control behavior, and do everything in our power to change our spouse or children. As I have seen with numerous Christian couples and families, this is the primary cause of exhaustion, depression, and the hopeless sense of wanting to bail out of it all. When people spend their lives trying to transform their spouse and their kids, the natural result is tiredness, discouragement, and the desire to quit. Therefore, this book is more about learning the *right job*, and less about learning new techniques.

This first step is easy—if we will do it: We must learn the simple difference between God's job and ours. God knows you have done the best you could, using the tools you've had. But God may be like Chrissy's father, saying to you, "I can see that you've worked really hard to help me and to please me. But—I don't quite know how to tell you this—you have been burning yourself out doing a job I never meant for you to do. You're trying to paint over something that's bound to break down in the end, and no amount of white paint can cover the mess. Let me show you how to build something that's brand-new."

I am talking about learning how to be continually empowered by God's grace, and therefore able to empower your spouse and children to learn and to grow. And to do that, we have to take the frightening step of giving up our fear of people and our drive to conform outwardly to what other Christians expect of us (or seem to).

God's job is to fix and to change. Our job is to depend, serve, and equip. This is the work of grace. And it is more restful than you can imagine.

As you change your mind about what your job really is, you are going to discover that you are more capable as a spouse or parent than you thought you were. You don't have to keep fixing those old relationships, even though it seems you have spent most of your life working on them. God and you can build anew with the people you love, relationships that will let in fresh air and light.

While this book contains many practical examples, it is *not* a "how-to" book. This is about God's grace. It is not possible to have truly healthy Christian families unless behaviors and attitudes are developed in the context of relationships that are grace-full, lived in an atmosphere of grace. My purpose, then, is to place the filter of

14

God's grace over the processes of marriage and parenting, the nuts and bolts of which may look different in each family.

Capable, creative, contented people, people of faith and depth, come from families where grace is in place. Isn't this what we all want?

Let's begin rethinking our relationship job by looking, in Part One, at families where grace is *not* in place—good Christian families where there is the sense that something is not "working right." It is for these families that I want to tell what I have learned, personally and professionally, about living in a family where grace is in place— and the rest and happiness that it brings.

1. Our Detour From God's Plan

Jack and Joan nervously took their seats at opposite ends of the couch. They had been married for six years—and dissatisfied for five. Their marriage was characterized by the word *survival*. The past twelve months had brought one crisis after another. I began with a seemingly non-volatile question. "Why did you come to see me?"

The next half hour consisted of one person trying to answer the question and the other interrupting with corrections, clarifications, and explanations. Their frustration levels grew as they took turns defending themselves against each other.

At the end of our session, I gave them an assignment to complete and bring back. They were to answer the question: *How would things have to be made different in order for you to become a happy person?* It was a question I'd had to struggle with myself years before.

Early in my own marriage the same question was posed to me by a Christian counselor. I remember sitting there listening to my wife's answer. As Holly verbalized her list, almost every item indicated a way in which I was not being adequate as a husband. I already felt like I wasn't much of a husband, and as her list grew I felt strangely more tired and more indicted. When it was my turn I gave the counselor my list, which not so coincidentally focused on my wife. And while it felt good to finally get in my digs, I felt sad for Holly: Her face registered shame with every verbal blow, every confirmation of her defectiveness as a wife.

"Look at the other person's list," the counselor then instructed us. "What are some ways you can do these things for each other?" Holly and I left our session with instructions to return the next week, each with a plan for how we were going to try harder to do and be what the other needed. I felt so discouraged.

Now in the role of counselor, I wondered what Jack and Joan would say when they returned to my office. A week later, each was armed with a manifesto describing how they would like their spouse to be different. I did not ask them the question our counselor had asked us years before, the one that had placed such a burden on already tired people. Instead, I asked, "How are you going to be a happy person even if the other person does not change?"

I could tell by their expressions that both were totally baffled. In unison they almost shouted, "What?!"

I clarified, "What if the other person doesn't become the person you want them to be? Is it possible for you to be a happy person?"

This alternative had not occurred to either one of them.

From the beginning of their relationship, they had each looked for right behavior from the other as their source of happiness. They were preoccupied with each other's "successes" and "failures." They had used a lot of energy trying to get each other to change.

To make matters more sticky, along with the mundane, the lists were loaded with very right-sounding spiritual tasks. "I want him to pray with me." "She should submit to me when I make a decision and stop making 'helpful suggestions.' " "He should . . ." "She should . . ."

Unfortunately, this dynamic seems to be the rule rather than the exception for the couples and parents who have sought my help. In striving to make their homes happier and better places, they have turned them into hellish places where people sense they can never measure up. The place that is to be a blessing begins to feel like a curse. God never intended our marriages and our homes to be this way. He had a sweeter plan. Before we go any further, we need to examine God's original plan for our intimate relationships.

GOD'S PLAN: ONE FLESH

What was the garden of Eden like before the incident with the forbidden fruit? Such a rich account of God-to-human and human-to-human relationships can be seen in Genesis 1–3. Genesis 1:26–28 tells of God's creation of humankind in His own likeness: It took both male and female in order to truly represent the likeness of God. (This is reiterated in Genesis 5.)

The "man" was in charge, but the man to whom responsibility was given—to be fruitful, fill the earth, subdue it, and rule over every living thing—was both male and female. So this is the first aspect of God's original plan for marriage: for males and females to be co-rulers, co-subduers.

God said, "It is not good for the man to be alone; I will make him a helper suitable for him" (Genesis 2:18). It does not say that God gave the man an assistant to order around. Beasts of the earth were to be ruled over—but this helper had to be "suitable" for the man. She had to "correspond to" him, to be in partnership with him. So God caused Adam to fall asleep and then God "fashioned" Eve (2:22). God created Eve. The language conveys something carefully and intentionally arranged on the part of God. Adam was formed, but Eve was fashioned—suitable, corresponding to.

Pay close attention to Adam's first response when he awoke and saw Eve: "This is now bone of my bones, and flesh of my flesh"

(v. 23). He did not say, "Great, now I have someone to get my stuff for me, do the chores I don't feel like doing, and cater to my every need." And the Word of God goes on: "For this cause a man shall leave his father and his mother, and shall cleave to his wife; and they shall become one flesh" (v. 24). This was God's plan for marriage: entering into the process of becoming one flesh. It is not to "subdue" or to "rule over" each other. Rather, the plan for marriage is a dependence upon God; two becoming one flesh, co-ruling, a relationship in the image of God.

How did we get so far off the mark?

GOD'S PLAN GETS SIDETRACKED

In one nightmarish moment everything for Adam, Eve, and the rest of humankind changed. Once they were dependent upon and in communion with God: Then came rebellion, shame, and hiding. What had been "one flesh" changed into disunity and blaming. Let me illustrate this visually:

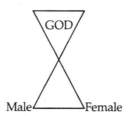

While Adam and Eve lived in a relationship with God in which they were dependent upon Him as the only One who could give life and meet all their needs, they needed to make no demands of each other. Looking only to Him they reflected His image.

Then the serpent convinced them they could do a better job of being God than God. He convinced them to depend upon themselves instead of God as their source. According to the serpent's thinking, control was better than dependence. In his opinion, the diagram should have looked like this:

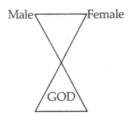

Unfortunately, Adam and Eve cooperated with this plan and disobeyed God. They sinned (missed the mark) in their attempt to be gods and to meet their own needs. How sad and unnecessary. They already had a God who was faithful, loving, and eager to give them everything they would ever need. Their choices and the ramifications of those choices resulted in what we know as the fall. And the following picture is what that looked like:

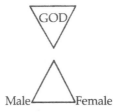

How does this bit of theology really affect you and me today—as husbands, wives, and parents?

DISTORTED RELATIONSHIPS

After the fall, we see how drastically things changed. Adam and Eve became afraid of God and wanted to hide from Him. In relationship to themselves as individuals they carried shame. And in relationship to each other, they began to blame and condemn.

But there is an even more serious ramification affecting male/female relationships. In Genesis 3, we find what is traditionally called the *curse*. In this passage, God said to the woman, "Your desire shall be for your husband, and he shall rule over you" (v. 16). First came the impulse to blame. Then God simply revealed the self-centered core that began to motivate each of them: The woman would continue to try to draw life and nurturing from a man who was not capable of filling these deep needs—never was and never will be. And the man would be forever trying to rule over the woman, either aggressively or passively trying to keep her quiet about his inadequacy to fill her needs. Each would demand love, respect, nurturing from the other. And as the generations of their children passed, men and women would forget that they were never supposed to draw their life from each other.

The concepts of "desire for" in a woman-to-man direction and "rule over" in a man-to-woman direction are seen in the final diagram:

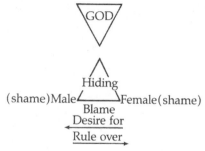

THE CURSE

What we see in Adam and Eve—and in Jack and Joan, Jeff and Holly—is the curse. It is not God's plan. His intent was that we rule together, dependent upon Him, mirroring His triune image in the way we relate in love to each other. This is not at all what the relationships look like in Genesis 3. When God said, "Your desire will be for your husband," the phrase He used is the same one He employed in warning Cain about the ravages of jealousy and rebellion. In Genesis 4:7 God said, "If you do well, will not your countenance be lifted up? And if you do not do well, sin is crouching at the door; and its *desire* is *for* you, but you must master it." Sin's desire is destructive, dominating, and usurping. Likewise, under the curse, the man would desire to "rule over" the woman. Sin would make the man tend to be harsh, despotic, and tyrannical in his leadership.

Curse is an excellent word for what is going on here. The resulting relationship is one where we see two people who, because of their struggling, are both over someone and under someone. And once they lock themselves in a battle for control, they are caught in a hellish trap. This is the curse in operation—it looks a lot like the marriage between Joan and Jack, and so many others. Instead of grace-full relationships, they have one that is *curse-full*. To me, the word *curse-full* means a relationship, or aspects of a relationship, characterized by "placing yourself over" another. The result is a set of relationship dynamics that are the very hallmarks of the curse. I am referring, of course, to every aspect of dominance and control, however carefully mastered in spiritualized terms, whether passive and subtle or aggressive and obvious.

CURSE-FULL RELATIONSHIPS BETWEEN PARENTS AND CHILDREN

"Hello," said the voice on the phone, "this is Dean Johnson from the college. It seems we're having another problem with Steve. Can you and your husband find a time when we can meet?" This was the fourth such call that Chad and Fran had received. They felt confused and tired. As I looked at them, sitting with their son Steve in my office, I noticed that this couple looked a tad angry as well.

The dean of the Christian college their son was attending had called to tell them Steve was caught drinking alcohol in his dorm room. As a result Steve was suspended. For years Chad and Fran had tried every way they knew to stop their son's drinking. But Steve insisted on breaking the rules set forth by the college and by his own family. His folks were understandably tired—but evidently not tired enough.

"You are going to stop acting this way!" Chad shouted, his voice seething with rage and hurt.

"I don't have to listen to you!" Steve shot back.

"Oh no? Well, I'm going to *make* you stop drinking if it's the last thing I do," Chad threatened. "You are embarrassing me, and you're hurting your mother."

"You can't order me around anymore," Steve taunted.

Can you see it? Here are two people, both of whom are trapped in the fruitless effort to dominate or win the other over to their side. And in their struggle to dominate they are actually focused upon— indeed locked into—a sick relationship. And so the curse spreads throughout all family relationships, unless we recognize that it is in operation and begin to seek a way to cut off its source of power.

OUR RESPONSE TO THE CURSE

There are thousands of sermons, hundreds of books, and scores of seminars designed to help Christians rid themselves of the curse, as if it were a scab that could be picked off the surface of the skin. I cannot make this point strongly enough: *It is not our job as Christians to carry out the curse.* God has given us a new plan. That plan, which is meant to set us free, is not powered by a "more spiritualized" means of dominating: That is, only splashing white paint over an old and deadly spirit of legalism. God's plan is powered by *grace*—that is, He has made available to us the power to be transformed from the inside out, and the power to guide others in our own families as they discover the path of inner transformation too.

It is not our job to perform the curse more nicely, or in a more spiritual way than the rest of the world does. It is our wonderful freedom to grow in relationships that carry out God's plan.

For most of us, the first step is something like detoxification. We have thought for so long that it is our job to make goodness happen in others that we can no longer see how we have slipped into our old controlling, curse-full style of relating. Let's look now at how we unwittingly weave the curse into our dearest relationships, by examining in more detail the characteristics of curse-full relationships.

DISCUSSION QUESTIONS

1. *Have you ever considered how you will be a happy person even if your spouse never changes? What are some factors that determine happiness for you? Explain.*[*1]

2. *Why do you think many couples think their happiness depends on how their spouse acts or reacts?*

3. *What do you think about the plan that God wants us to get our happiness primarily from Him?*

4. *How do we tend to live our lives under "the curse" rather than according to God's plan? What does that look like in your family?[*]*

5. *What is the reason why we usually want to control the actions of others, especially family members?*

---

[1] Questions marked with an asterisk are for individuals or couples only.

2. Curse-Full Relationships

"My husband, Rick, doesn't seem to care about spiritual things. He's never read the Bible, and it's getting harder and harder to get him to go to church. What bothers me most is that he's setting a bad example for the kids." So began my session with Danine several years ago.

"How can I help you?" I began—meaning, "How can I help you with *you*?"

It was immediately apparent that she thought it was her job to control Rick's behavior. So what she heard me ask was, "How can I help you get your husband to act more spiritual?" This was evident by her answer: "For starters, I've been getting him up and out the door for church for ten years now and I'm running out of tricks. I was hoping you could help me think of some new ways to motivate him."

Whose responsibility is Rick's spirituality? It is Rick's. Whose had it become? Danine's. She had taken on the task of trying to control

Rick's church attendance, Scripture reading, and the example he was for the kids. No wonder she was getting tired.

The original curse resulted when Adam and Eve took their eyes off God, who is our primary Source. Today, the curse is played out in relationships as a result of the very same mistake: In a curse-full marriage, one partner makes demands on the other as if he/she were the source rather than a *resource*. Danine was trying to get her needs met from Rick's spiritual activity. And when Rick did not perform, Danine wrongly assumed it was her job to see that his spiritual needs were met. Chapters 3, 4, and 5 will show the phases through which relationships pass as a result of this type of dynamic. For now, let's examine the characteristics of curse-full relationships.

C.U.R.S.E.

Danine and Rick's story illustrates one distinct trait of curse-full relationships. Curse-full relationships have many characteristics, and the one that we will focus on here is our underlying tendency to usurp God's role by trying in futile and powerless ways to *control*. To help us see this more clearly, I will develop my thoughts around the acronym—C.U.R.S.E. Each letter happens to stand for a primary aspect of curse-full relationships. They are:

C — Controlling
U — Unforgiving
R — Reactive
S — Shaming
E — Ego-Driven

Controlling

If our sense of well-being and value come from the behavior of another person instead of God, we will always be giving off messages that say to others: You'd better perform right. The innate problem is that no human being is capable of performing well enough to establish another's self-esteem—that person's behavior will always fall short at some point. If the other person is not willing or able to change their behavior fast enough or in the "right way" to meet our needs, most of us decide that their behavior is an issue we must do something about.

This is what happened with Danine. She accepted the job of directing Rick's behavior. When she sought my help, it was because she sensed that the job had gotten too big and she was failing. Therefore, she wanted extra muscle from me in her struggle to get Rick to straighten up and fly right. "Help me to fix and control my husband" was her plea. Yes, her concerns were legitimate—but she had unwittingly stepped into the wrong role in Rick's process of spiritual growth.

Let me state this clearly: It is all well and good for Danine to care about her husband's spirituality. It is right for her to be concerned and to feel frustrated that Rick does not seem to care about God. What is destructive, however, to Rick, Danine, and ultimately their relationship, are her attempts to control and the struggles they always trigger. With Danine in control of Rick's actions, Rick did not have to learn to be in charge of himself. And he did not have to face the consequences of his spiritual stagnation, because Danine had managed for ten years to make Rick *look* as if he were in better spiritual shape than he really was.

This same dynamic can be seen in many different relationship settings: A husband can try to control his alcoholic wife's drinking by pouring out her booze. A pastor can try to control his congregation's giving by promising them prosperity. Parents try to control the grades of their children by shaming and comparing them to others. A child tries to control his/her parents' temper by being perfect. A wife tries to control her husband's attacks by zeroing out her needs, her will, and her personality, and being "submissive." A Christian attempts to control God's view of him/her by trying to be holy. If we do not understand the operations of grace, then the curse is free to reign everywhere—even in the body of Christ.

In John 21, Jesus gives Peter an indication of the kind of death the apostle was going to die. Peter, surrounded by his fellow disciples, wanted to know what was in store for them:

> Peter, turning around, saw the disciple whom Jesus loved [John] following them; the one who also had leaned back on His breast at the supper . . . Peter therefore seeing him said to Jesus, "Lord, what about this man?" Jesus said to [Peter], "If I want him to remain until I come, what is that to you? You follow Me!"

As is often true with us, it was easier for Peter to focus on someone else's walk with Jesus than on his own. And while we are busy trying to correct and take charge of the spiritual lives of others, Jesus would remind us that the only relationship with the Lord we have to concern ourselves with is our own.

I am not at all advocating irresponsibility in our relationships. I am not suggesting parents shrug off their charge to raise their children in a godly manner. Rather, it is that we most often substitute manipulation, legalism, and shame when God has shown us another way. We will examine this in detail later.

Unforgiving

"Be kind to one another, tender-hearted, forgiving each other, just as God in Christ also has forgiven you" (Ephesians 4:32). That's what the apostle Paul says. But curse-full relationships are unforgiving.

If you've read many marriage books, you may have come across the concept of "fair fighting." One of the main ingredients in this success formula is the idea that, when trying to discuss a problem, it is not fair for either party to bring up things from the past. When I say that curse-full relationships are unforgiving, I am not simply talking about a lack of forgiveness for a given incident. I am talking about a lack of forgiveness for things that happened years and even decades before. This can be seen by the amount of time and energy used to rehash old issues for which there still is no forgiveness.

For some people, unforgiveness serves a very practical purpose. One reason why people don't or won't forgive is because it is a way for them to have the upper hand over another; it holds the other in a position of owing a debt they cannot repay. And feeling held in a constant state of being unforgiven keeps some people scrambling to discover what good behavior it will take on their part to make up for what they have done wrong. In a very real and devilish sense, unforgiveness becomes an effective tool to control another's behavior.

Reactive

People in curse-full relationships have not learned how freeing it is to *respond* to someone else's behavior. Healthy responses are based upon what is true, what is beneficial, and what is appropriate. People who are not free *react* in order to control the situation. When your sense of well-being comes from the performance of another, in fact, you are assigning that person a lot of power over you. Their words and behavior have power to indict or vindicate. The other person has the power to establish your self-esteem or to destroy it. Consequently, when that other person acts in a way that is bad "public relations" for you, you must react immediately in order to get on top of the situation. Under the curse the byword is *control* or be controlled.

What a sad contrast to Paul's description of love in 1 Corinthians 13! Paul says that love "is not provoked." This means that when we learn to rest in God's love, outside factors do not control our response—love does. Love is also patient—which means slow to anger—but curse-full relationships are often full of angry reactions

30

of either the icy or heated varieties. In either case, love frees—while living under the curse traps us in our own reactions.

Shaming

Shame is the painful sense that you lack value as a person. It is the belief that you are defective, worthless, unlovable. It is not simply that something is wrong with your behavior, it is that something is wrong with you as a person.[1]

Shame is often used by people as a means of placing themselves over others. When I give you the message that you are bad or defective, I am placing myself in the position of being more valuable, or more powerful, and the judge of your value as a person. Shame is also used in an attempt to control the behavior of others.

How would you respond, for example, if someone said, "What's wrong with you—why can't you be like your brother?" If you react by trying harder to be like your brother, then that person has succeeded in shaming you—that is, playing on a sense of defectiveness—and controlled you to change your behavior to escape the feeling of worthlessness.

Or, what if someone said to you, "The Lord is not happy with your lack of giving to the church (monetarily)." If you gave more, it would not be a result of loving God and trusting His faithfulness to meet your needs. You would only be reacting to the shame you felt, and you would be performing more *spiritual-looking* behavior for someone else.

In the context of family relationships, suppose your spouse said, "What kind of husband/wife are you anyway?" If you changed your behavior, it would most likely be an attempt to escape the indictment, or to protect yourself from being indicted again.

---

[1] For a more complete discussion on shame and its effects on the Christian, please refer to *Tired of Trying to Measure Up* (Minneapolis: Bethany House, 1990).

In all the above cases, you would be motivated more by fear than by love.

Ego-Driven

As I have said before, the tip-off that the curse is what drives a relationship is this dynamic: One person places himself over others, on top of the pile.

People in curse-full relationships are ego-driven. (That is the fancy psychological equivalent of being selfish.) Beneath their line of conscious, or stated, reasoning lies another layer of thought, where the truth is hidden:

- I want my children to dress a certain way because of what people will think of *me*.
- I want my spouse to go to church because of what people might say about *me*, if he/she doesn't go.
- I need you to cater to me so *I* can feel important.
- For you to want to do something other than what I want means *I* must not matter to you.
- For you to give someone else attention instead of me means something is wrong with *me*.

Behaviors in these relationships are so ego-driven that even apparent selflessness masks underlying selfish motives:

- I must please my spouse in every way and meet every need so *I* can feel like a good spouse.
- I must speak kindly to my children in public so others will see me as a good parent.
- I must never say no when asked to do something in the church, so others will see me as a dedicated Christian.

What does it feel like to live in a curse-full relationship? The following acronym describes it well.

T.I.R.E.D.

In my experience as a counselor, Christians wait too long to ask for help. And when they finally do, it is usually because they are tired. I mean emotionally, mentally, and spiritually drained. They have tried and tried, and one day they realize they are exhausted, and all of their trying has not helped!

Picture the word *tired* if you want to remember the primary signals that indicate when you are operating under the curse:

> T — Trapped
> I — Indicted
> R — Responsible
> E — Exposed
> D — Defensive

Trapped

If you are part of a curse-full relationship, you are living in a *no-win* situation. No matter how well you perform, it will never be good enough. You know how tired and sad you feel. You are disillusioned and confused because this hasn't turned out the way you thought it would. It would be easier to just disappear. But you can't, because you also know what God says about divorce. You feel trapped, as if you have been sentenced to this relationship. It feels like a trick.

Indicted

In the course of living under the curse, you have been reminded over and over that you are inadequate. *Maybe something really is wrong with you.* Sometimes you feel that you don't even *like* this person you're supposed to love. You feel like a bad person, a bad partner, a bad Christian. What is wrong with you?

Responsible

You feel responsible for everything and everyone. You know how sad and tired your partner is, and it's your fault. You have an overwhelming sense of how responsible you are for the state of his/her relationship. You may even feel responsible for God's mood, as you envision Him looking in on your relationship.

Exposed

Living in a curse-full relationship means having someone else focus on your behavior, scrutinizing your every move. You feel exposed and vulnerable and dirty. The place that is supposed to be the safest—your home, your relationship—becomes the least safe.

Defensive

As a result of all of this, you are defensive. In order to fend off the constant indictments, you maintain an air of being right, even when you know you are wrong. You learn to attack the other person first because the best defense is a good offense. And all the while, you sense that you are becoming more and more distant from this person you love. But to let down your guard may leave you unprotected. Better to keep him/her at a distance.

Most people who feel worn out in a relationship think they are tired because of the other person. "If he would just change," or "If she would only stop pressuring me, I wouldn't be so tired." *This is not true!* You and I are the cause of our own tiredness, by trying to make changes in someone else that we do not have the power to make.

I have just given you some diagnostic information to help you discern if the relationships in your home are curse-full. In the following chapter we will look at some phases that are common in relationships when the curse takes over and pushes out God's gracefull plan.

DISCUSSION QUESTIONS

1. *Name some ways you live under "the curse" in your family relationships.**

2. *Why is unforgiveness damaging to family relationships? Give some examples.*

3. *Have you ever felt trapped in a relationship? Why? Do you think it had something to do with your expectations? Explain.*

3. Living Under the Curse

Not all of the marriage situations I see are exactly the same, of course, but in *all* marriage relationships that are under stress or breaking down there are several common denominators. I will "animate" these factors by allowing you to see them at work in a typical case study.

EMPTINESS CEMENTED

Jan comes from a background of family relationships like the ones described in the previous chapter—relationships where there is pressure for outward conformity with no loving empowerment for true, lasting inner growth and change.

If a family has a history of curse-full, performance-oriented relationships, we can be certain of several unhappy results. In Jan's case she carries a deeply ingrained sense of shame, or defectiveness. Jan also learned to perform in many ways to cover her shame. Unfortunately, her efforts have failed to erase the feeling of defectiveness—in fact, by working harder she has set herself up for failure.

Jan took on more church duties, and obligated herself to numerous school activities. She also determined to live up to the fruit of the Spirit list—to be loving, patient, kind ... Imagine her sense of failure when she didn't perform well in any one of these areas. As a result, with each slip, failure, sin, omission, or *faux pas,* her sense of defectiveness was highlighted. It was crushing. If she could have drawn a picture of herself—a self that felt like a zero—it would have looked like this:

From every relationship, Jan was trying to draw a sense of worth, nurturing, and inner life.

PERFORMANCE AFFIRMED

Unfortunately for Jan—and for most of us—most relationships reinforce our performance orientation. We understand that our acceptance is conditional, and that it is necessary for us to perform. Though Jan never thought of her relationships this way, her *training* told her it was true. Obviously, the people in her church, family, and community had been trained with a strong performance orientation too. Most of the people in our world will project this message to us, as they projected it to Jan: You must earn love and acceptance in order to establish your value.

The result is the dichotomy represented in the following diagram. Notice that we may feel and look full as pertaining to our outer behavior, but still feel the desperate need of something or someone to fill us on the inside:

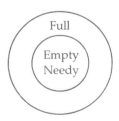

This is the true state of our souls. They are empty, needy, and in search of life and worth.

CONDITIONED TO BE IDOLATROUS

Spiritually speaking, something other than performing has been learned. Jan, like the rest of us, has been deeply immersed in the curse. Therefore, she believes it is her job to control her behavior, the behavior of her husband and children—and to control others' opinion of her by regulating her behavior. Without knowing it at all, she is really trying to control *them*. A life of this has taught her several things:

- Don't make waves.

- Someone may not like how you feel, what you think, how you act—so be quiet.

- You are here to meet the needs of everyone else.

- Your needs are negotiable. In fact, you're selfish if you even *have* needs.

- What is real and true is not the most important thing. The most important thing is how things look and what people think.

Jan has been programmed with a radar system that hones in on the opinions, reactions, and the performance of others. Underneath is a desperate drive to be in control. How things look has become the primary concern in most of her relationships. Therefore, issues of genuine personal fullness and health are seldom, if ever, raised. In fact, Jan feels selfish when she even thinks about her own needs. In effect, she has been conditioned, by virtue of her own neediness, to move toward and to lean on dependent relationships with people or positions. If she were to face the truth, it is this: Living this way is idolatrous.

In an idolatrous relationship, the well-being of one person is dependent upon the full performance of the other person. Let's take a look at the way this works in Jan's marriage.

A MARRIAGE MADE IN HEAVEN?

Very often, needy, empty-feeling people are drawn toward someone who is just like them. Both, in fact, sense emptiness on the inside, while their performance signals they are full. That is because the emptiness of each person so desperately needs the full performance of the other. And since they have been taught that how things *look* is all-important, the behavior of the other person looks very promising! That full-looking exterior promises to meet those needs that were left unmet in previous relationships. It looks like this:

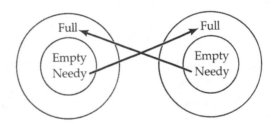

The line with the arrow represents the ways in which the emptiness of one person looks at the external performance of the other, wrongly believing this person will be the source of their own sense of well-being or fullness.

When Jan married Tony, he was a successful young manager in a local company, attended Bible studies with her, and volunteered his help with the church youth group. He made no demands on her at all. He was like a knight in shining armor. She could not imagine that, deep inside, Tony was working hard to prove himself as a man and as an acceptable Christian. He just performed very well.

I cannot overemphasize this fact: Empty people cannot fill other empty people. They merely *look* as though they can fill empty people.

From the outset, this was a marriage headed for big potholes in the road of life—the kind of relationship that keeps a lot of marriage counselors in business.

CODEPENDENCY

Christians balk at the term *codependency*. In a way, this is a right reaction. Too often, the word *codependency* has been used to speak only of the psychological aspects of human relationships. Christians must know there is a deeper level at which we must learn to live, a level where spiritual principles operate, and where our relationship to God must be considered. As Christians, we are members of a spiritual family, with God as our Father; He cannot be left out of our figuring—or our counseling. Let's consider how this works in Jan and Tony's marriage.

Actually, what Jan and Tony have growing here is not a real relationship—it's a psychological arrangement, and a spiritually idolatrous dependency. The *addictiveness* of the relationship, on the psychological level, can be seen by looking at each person's preoccupation with the other's performance. Much like an alcoholic who is preoccupied with alcohol, or the workaholic who is preoccupied with his work, both Jan and Tony were focused on another person's behavior. If Jan was up and happy, Tony felt that he was doing a good job as a husband. If she was down, he worked hard trying to make her happy and relaxed again. Jan was in the same trap with Tony and his moods and actions.

This is codependency. I have written an entire book on addiction and codependency.[1] But I want you to know that codependency not only occurs in families where there is an alcoholic, it happens in any situation where a performance standard is more important than real psychological *and* spiritual need. In a relationship like this, people

---

[1] See Jeff VanVonderen, *Good News for the Chemically Dependent and Those Who Love Them* (Minneapolis: Bethany House, 1995).

become codependent, depending on each other's performance for their sense of well-being and validity.

In my early days of counseling, I must admit I was very reluctant to diagnose a person as codependent unless we could find a dependent person in his/her life. Actually, most of the people I have counseled that are now struggling with codependency were codependent *before* they ever met their dependent loved one. They had learned performance-reward behavior in their family of origin.

Also, there is a "feel" about the word *codependency* that makes it sound like a second-class issue, not really as serious as dependency. This is wrong. Codependency *is* dependency, probably more prevalent than chemical dependency and every bit as difficult to overcome.

RESCUING EQUITY

When Jan's "radar" detects even a hint that Tony is down, or that he has a bad attitude, or is doing something wrong, one of two things usually happens inside Jan.

The first seems rather ironic. She sometimes ignores or denies the incident and concludes that there is something wrong with her own radar. She decides that it must be her own wrong perception of the situation. This is not unusual in light of the unwritten rules Jan grew up with: Do not notice when someone else fails; if you do notice, *you* are the problem.

The second response is more normal for Jan. She will do something in an attempt to correct Tony's negative behavior or attitude. She is convinced that she can change Tony by working hard enough on her own.

The addictive nature of the relationship grows because both Jan and Tony choose to keep investing time, energy, and emotions in the relationship in order to rescue past investments—that is, all the hard work they've put into building this lovely and superficial relationship.

To stop trying to change the other person's behavior—to stop trying to fill the other's emptiness—would be to admit that they have wasted many years and lots of energy. Their failure to control things by trying hard would also further underscore their already ingrained sense of defectiveness. It's easier to avoid the shame of failure by controlling the addictive behavior.

And besides, how would it look? What would people think? After all, appearance is what matters, not the fact that this is an empty relationship. Therefore, it would be easier to continue pouring more into the relationship in hopes of future improvement. I have seen people, for instance, who have gotten married to rescue four years of lousy dating! The result was just a more permanent version of that unhealthy relationship.

AN AVERAGE CASE

At this point, I would like to give you a description of a typical first marriage-counseling session. Jan and Tony enter the office and I ask, "Why have you come? How can I help?"

Jan was readily able to tell me a list of the things that are not working in the marriage, those things for which they needed help. Tony told me that the reason he was there was because Jan made him come.

"What would have to change in order for you to be happy?" I asked Jan. "What would it take for you to feel secure?"

She thought. Then came a long list of behaviors Tony would have to change.

"If he would stop blowing up at me when I mention something that's bothering me . . . Like the way he keeps missing our weekly Bible study group. He never used to. It worries me that he's not living up to the commitment we made to these people. Or when he buys something for himself that costs a lot of money. It's not that he doesn't work hard and *deserve* it. But . . . well, we were taught as young Christians to make these decisions together. It makes me feel left out—and like . . . well, maybe Tony is bailing out of our commitment to each other . . ."

And the list went on. Always, Tony had missed a high mark they had aimed for. And always, Jan took it to mean that his "failure" meant he didn't love her as he used to—and therefore something was defective about her. The bottom line was that Tony's outer performance was interpreted to mean Jan was as worthless as she felt. Of course, she did not see that her sense of worthlessness was there all along.

Turning to Tony, I asked the same question: "What would have to change for you to be happy?" His response was typical of husbands: "If my wife would get off my case, everything would be fine. I don't know what the big deal is! If she would just *be* okay, everything would be okay. Things just aren't that bad."

Eventually, Tony did admit that he was tired of trying to figure out what Jan wanted, and getting fed up with feeling as if he could never please her.

THOSE HURTFUL LISTS

If I left the story at this point, I could be accused of reinforcing some stereotypes about men and women—stereotypes that I think are incorrect and not at all helpful. Actually, the reason wives more often have a longer list than their husbands is not because women are oversensitive or domineering. Sometimes that *is* the case, and that is a different issue. Nor is the wife's long list due to the husband's *insensitivity.* Many times a husband is not aware of what is happening in the marriage because he has been trained to keep his emotions in check and at a shallow level. He can be out of touch with deeper feelings, even oblivious to pain in a relationship.

Sometimes husbands are not willing to defend themselves by writing their own list. And in our society, men respond to the screams of the boss, not to those of the wife.

But what is more dangerous and destructive about the *list approach* is not the length of the list but that there is a list at all. The wife's list, no matter how long or short, communicates to the husband, "I don't like you. I don't accept you. But if you perform the way I think you should, *then* I will like and accept you." And no matter how long the husband's list may be, it says in like manner to his wife, "I don't like you either. But if you stop caring about things so much, if you stop feeling the way you feel and noticing the things you notice, then I will accept and like you."

And so, the relationship that God has provided as a grace-full resource, which could affirm both of these people, is full of strings attached, and it communicates rejection and the message: "You are defective. Perform!"

MARRIAGE PROBLEMS DON'T DEVELOP OVERNIGHT

Marriage relationships don't break down overnight. A couple does not wake up one morning and suddenly discover that their marriage isn't working. Inevitably, by the time a married couple hits the sofa in a counselor's office, they have waited far too long to get help sorting things out and healing the relationship.

In the early stages of marriage, both partners are full of energy, enthusiasm, and idealism. They are going to have the best marriage there ever was, the marriage their parents never had. He's going to be the best husband there ever was, and she will be the best wife. They're going to learn from the mistakes of their parents, and *do it right*! They are not going to let happen to them what happened to "so-and-so." Maybe they even want to have a business or ministry together someday.

After a few years of the best marriage that self-effort, people-pleasing, and stuffing pain can buy, trying hard begins to wear a little thin. It gets harder and harder to pretend you don't feel the way you really feel. It gets more and more difficult to overlook what the other person does that drives you bananas. It's not as easy to keep focusing on the needs and feelings of others at the expense of your own. You're tired of walking on eggshells all the time to protect people's feelings and opinions. Honesty? Integrity? Vulnerability? Who even knows what these are about?

Admitting the presence of a problem in your marriage is murder, because you have invested your energy into earning acceptance from your positive exterior. You have spent so much time grooming the opinions of your parents, friends, people at church, or even your own children concerning your put-together Christian life and your put-together Christian marriage that it's very hard indeed to admit the truth. "Maybe it would just be easier to go on pretending, at least until the kids leave home."

Or maybe you are like some others I've seen. One day it occurs to them that losing the marriage would be a worse assault on their self-esteem than acknowledging the problem. So after waiting and waiting and waiting, and despite the shame of admitting they need help, they finally come to their pastor or counselor.

TRYING HARD IS NOT THE RIGHT ANSWER

Even if it is done right, learning to have a healthy marriage relationship is a complicated, messy process. In Jan and Tony's case, it's going to be even messier. Some people have shame so deeply ingrained into their identity, and they have become experts in performing and in getting others to perform in order to cover the shame. Unhealthy patterns for trying to earn love and acceptance are such a part of their very fiber that these things are hard even to recognize, let alone change.

If trying hard was the key to a healthy marriage, most couples would find themselves in the *Healthy Marriage Hall of Fame* instead of in counseling. So trained are we to the formula-mentality that most couples who come for counseling expect to receive one more recipe for a successful marriage. They've read the experts. They've done the *seminar shuffle.* They know Dr. So-and-So's secret marriage formula by heart. Most counseling clients come to me, therefore, wanting *my* plan—the fix, something more to do: "Jeff's Ten Steps to a Victorious Christian Marriage."

Trying hard is not the answer. But if you've been in a relationship like the one just described, you already know that. You've probably tried everything more than once. I hope you are ready to accept that the painful truth can also be the wonderful beginning of the big turnaround you are hoping for: Trying hard is not the answer.

So far I've given you an overview of a curse-full relationship. In the next two chapters we will take an even closer look. I think you will recognize not only yourself and your mistakes but also the beginning of a new and healthy life you can bring to your marriage and family relationships, starting now.

DISCUSSION QUESTIONS

1. *Why do you think you or someone you know takes on more and more responsibilities outside the home—particularly at church?*

2. *Have you ever been told or felt that your own needs were not a consideration? Explain. Do you think they should be?*

3. *What does a codependent relationship look like?*

4. *What danger do you see in making lists of things your spouse is not doing, or doing incorrectly?*

5. *Why is trying harder not the answer in a troubled relationship?*

4. When a Marriage Doesn't Work

Mark was one of the most dedicated Christian men I'd ever met. In the community, he had a sterling reputation as a business and civic leader; in his church, he was a hardworking deacon and an excellent Sunday school teacher. In large part, his apparent success at everything he put his hand to came from a "can do" attitude. He often sacrificed his own comfort and needs to help someone else or to work for some higher goal. When problems came up for his wife and kids, Mark directed them to what he always did: "Quit complaining—when you focus on a problem, you become a problem. Just do the right thing. It doesn't matter whether you like it or not. The kingdom of God is not a democracy."

One day, reality gave Mark an alarming wake-up call. His wife, Karin, began to suffer symptoms of a breakdown and checked herself into a local health clinic. Mark received the emergency call at work. He rushed to her bedside and, holding her hand, tried to offer comfort. "You can lick this, hon. I don't know what's happening here, but if you'll just call on the Lord—"

Karin exploded. "Look at me, Mark! *Look at me.* Do you see what's happening to me? Have you ever *really* seen me—or what I need? Do you really know the kids, or what they need? I didn't marry you to have an 'answer man.' And if you tell me one more time, 'Just pray about it,' I'll go over the edge. Stop giving us your mechanical answers, and *love* us." Tears of frustration that had been building—for years—finally choked off her plea.

Two of their three children had come to the clinic with Karin. Their eyes, full of tears, met his—and all Mark could see, suddenly, belatedly, was the depth of pain they carried, pain he'd stifled in them. All he could hear in his mind were the years of Christian principles he'd cited to his family—the standards Christians were supposed to live up to in order to be good Christians. Had he been wrong somehow, even while he was speaking the "right" words? On the other hand, maybe this was just some kind of spiritual attack.

Mark's twelve-year-old daughter was sobbing too hard to speak. But his teenaged son looked him in the eye and, in the most impassioned voice Mark had ever heard, pleaded with him. "Dad, we love you. But you make us feel like we're never going to be good enough. Please listen to what Mom's saying. *Help her!*"

As Mark later told me, his son's plea led him to a watershed decision: Once they got Karin through this crisis, he had to reexamine the way he was living his Christian life. He still believed with all his heart that the Bible was true—but there was something missing in the way he'd been taught to apply biblical principles. As he said when he called to set up the appointment, "It's like I learned the letter of the law, but the Spirit is missing. I thought that only happened in Old Testament lives—but I think I've been a pretty legalistic New Testament Christian. I don't know how it happened. What am I missing?"

The more I got to know Mark, the more I could understand his confusion. He was a good father and husband in many senses of the word. Above all, he loved Karin and the kids. He wanted them to learn Christian-living principles because he loved God and believed that Christianity is the best thing going.

Eventually, both he and Karin came to understand the major source of the relationship breakdown had occurred long before it showed up in Karin's physical and emotional collapse. Even though Karin had become a consumate pretender, nevertheless she was more often aware of relationship stress, and more likely to experience actual physical and emotional symptoms when pain and needs were ignored. Because Mark really is a compassionate man, he was willing to listen deeply to Karin's heart-needs for the first time so he could understand where he'd taken a wrong turn in the path.

And because of his willing-to-learn attitude, this is the conclusion he himself voiced after not too many sessions: "I always thought I was doing the loving and right thing by directing my family just to act on godly principles. I thought that *doing* and *obedience* were the simple answers to all our needs and problems. I just didn't see that I was making them perform right on the outside, while inside their hearts were still aching for some real compassion. If I'd given them the compassion first—as a foundation to stand on—they would have had more real power inside. I was really blind to the fact that I was just making them work real hard, without giving them emotional and spiritual fuel to get them through a day. Man, I really blew it."

Mark is only one of countless Christian men and women who have been taught by churches and seminar leaders that spiritual life results from performing according to certain principles. He had been taught to gauge spiritual success by outward performance standards, and had not been shown the internal steps that lead to real, *from-the-heart-out* empowerment and transformation. He had not been shown how to *live*.

As a result, Mark thought unsolved problems were proof he had failed as a Christian man, father, and husband. Whenever his wife and children sent out signals that communicated, "I can't do it," or

"I need help," he believed that his job as "the family problem-solver" was to find the right action for them to take to resolve the problem and encourage them to work hard at it. It is little wonder that many men like Mark, and especially their families, feel as though they are on an endless performance treadmill, with no rest in sight. Little wonder that so many Christians, in working harder to reach a solution, burn themselves out and, like Karin, nearly go over the edge.

Certainly, not every Christian who wants to grow in their commitment will wind up like Mark and Karin. In no way do I mean to suggest that. But when will we all wake up to the message: Solutions should build us up, not wear us out. And if our solutions are killing us, maybe it's time to change course.

THREE *CURSE-FULL* COURSES

On a fundamental level, most of us wrongly believe that we must work harder to overcome problems. And when problems continue, our answer is much like Mark's: "Work harder." But what happens when all our hard work fails?

There are several courses of action people choose in order to avoid the shaming admission that their self-effort is inadequate. In this chapter, we will focus on the various well-intended but curse-full courses of action a man or woman might choose to follow in trying to make his/her marriage work. Unfortunately, avoiding deeper issues or trying harder, which many Christian couples do, actually causes them to wait far too long to ask for help. In other words, choosing one of these alternatives postpones the solution.

1. Denying the Problem

If you are married, how long did you live with your spouse before you realized that your relationship wasn't working out the way you thought it would? Most people who come to me for counseling reply,

"Six months." It is significant to note that this tends to be the answer of people who have been married a year, five years, ten years, or forty years. How have they managed to get by, then, for the balance of the time when their relationship was in a state of breakdown?

The first alternative most of us choose is to *deny* the presence of the problem. Why do we do this? I'd like to suggest it is because most of us feel it is our job to keep each other happy by means of our good behavior, whether or not our partner gives us the real love and acceptance we need. We refuse to confront an issue because we might hurt the person or make him mad. We don't realize this is a sad effort to control the behavior or feelings of others. Depending on how long we can keep up the facade, the easiest way to maintain our false sense of peace is to deny the presence of a problem. This means we live in fundamental dishonesty, because untrue things are being said, and the true things, which need to be said, are treated as taboo.

So many complicating factors are at work here. Any time one partner in a marriage, for instance, sees a problem, *denial* trains them to say, inwardly: *I must be imagining it altogether. My "radar" must be defective.* Or they say, *There must be something about me that caused the problem in the first place.* Or, *what would people think?* Consequently, they will choose *not* to confront the issue. Of course, the problem is perpetuated. This relationship is held together on the basis of what is not said: This is denial.

Consider Danine, whom I introduced earlier, and who thought it was her Christian duty to keep her husband, Rick, going to church. The truth was this: Rick didn't really want to go to church. He didn't want to go to the Friday night Bible study. In fact, he didn't really care about God at all. But Danine thought it was her job to get him to care. She had tried, she was tired, and she wanted me to help her do her job. What follows is the rest of our conversation:

JEFF: Instead of going through two days of hinting, plotting, and bugging, why don't you simply inform Rick, in time for him to get ready, that you'll be leaving for church?

DANINE: What if he doesn't get ready?

JEFF: Then go without him.

DANINE: Well, what should I tell everyone who asks where he is?

JEFF: What have you been telling them so far?

DANINE: That he's sick, or out of town. Or anything I can think of.

JEFF: Why don't you tell them the truth?

DANINE: What—that Rick would rather stay home and watch professional wrestling?

JEFF: Is that the truth?

DANINE: Yes. That or cartoons!

JEFF: Well, tell them that.

DANINE: But if I told them that, what would people think?

JEFF: People would think what is true—that Rick cares more about professional wrestling than church.

DANINE: But how would that look?

JEFF: It would look like Rick cares about church as little as he really does. . . .

Danine had been living this way for many years, and doing so in order to control people's opinion of her husband. And, I think, to control their opinion of her as well. She was doing it out of a false understanding of submission, which she had learned from church leaders who told her (in subtle ways) that performance, not inner heart transformation, is what the Christian life is all about. By taking on responsibility for other people's perception of Rick's behavior, she was actually helping Rick stay home—the exact opposite of what she wished would happen. This is not true submission. This is called lying. True submission, on the other hand, is empowering or transforming.

I have heard painful reports from many people who *force* themselves to visit their families for the holidays. The reason it takes such a gargantuan effort for many people to visit their parents, siblings, or other family members is because it's very painful to be with them. Many people find themselves belittled, corrected, told what terrible parents they are, or find themselves on the losing end of comparisons.

I often ask, "Why don't you talk to your family about how hurtful their behavior is?" Here is a sampling of the replies:

"I don't want the relationship to be strained."

"That wouldn't be nice."

"That wouldn't be honoring to my parents."

And in response I want to say: "The relationships are already strained. Is it nicer to come up with new lies each year about why you can't visit? Is it somehow evil or unchristian simply to tell the truth, and then try to build the relationship? Do you think treating other adult family members like babies who are not capable of handling the truth is what *honoring* means? Many people do!"

Ephesians 4:25 says, "Laying aside falsehood, speak truth." Yet how many Christians refuse to speak the truth about hard or unpleasant issues in order to keep up a facade of peace, only to sacrifice true peace on the inside. One unhappy day they wake up and realize that there was never real peace on the outside either. A lot of people sacrifice their integrity and try to tiptoe around difficult family members, attempting to protect a "closeness" with them that doesn't even exist. No wonder people are tired.

2. Fixing the Other Person

The second alternative you might choose is to try to "fix" the behavior of your spouse. The fact that your peace and well-being depends on your spouse's performance leads us to an interesting point—one you may never have considered: If your peace and happiness depends on your spouse, then that person has become a false god to you. When your spouse is not performing up to your expectations, do you believe it is your job to fix his/her behavior? Then you will always live in a rut: You will always be working hard to restore your spouse to a level of "right" behavior, or lose all sense of calm and closeness. But the truth is the "peace" is only external and temporary. The relationship feels like a roller-coaster ride, with its highs coming from your self-effort and the other person's effort.

With the help of a diagram begun in the previous chapter, I want to show the dynamics of how a relationship functions when one member tries to fix the other person.

The first situation that can occur, when you depend on your spouse, is triggered when your spouse simply *lacks* those traits you desire. It means that your spouse is *inadequate* in your view. No one wants to believe their source of well-being is inadequate. Therefore, you respond by exerting some kind of pressure, hoping to cause your spouse to perform. You wrongly assume that this will meet your needs.

Here's what that dynamic looks like:

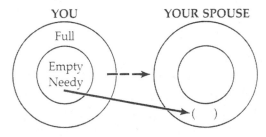

The solid line with the arrow represents the man or woman looking to the good performance of his/her spouse. The broken line with the arrow represents the pressure you exert to cause your spouse to perform a certain way. This can include nagging, pleading, manipulating, bribing, bargaining, yelling, hitting, threatening, quoting Bible verses, or quietly sulking. The parentheses indicate the behavior you are hoping to produce in response. Unfortunately, the space is empty: You will never get what you are hoping for because your spouse does not have the skill in him/her.

Notice how this works in the following examples.

> YOU: Why don't you talk to me? We never just sit and talk about things. You talk to your friends and family. Why don't you talk to me?
>
> SPOUSE: All right. Let's talk. What do you want to talk about? Pick a subject.
>
> YOU: Well, I shouldn't have to ask. Why do I have to make a big deal just to get you to talk to me? Before we were married we used to talk all the time. Now I can barely get a yes or no answer out of you.
>
> SPOUSE: See! When I don't talk to you I'm in trouble, and when I offer to talk to you I'm in trouble. Nothing I do pleases you.

Should people who are married spend time communicating with each other? Absolutely. But this scenario is not really about communicating. It's about meeting the needs of intimacy and attention. But more than that, it's about expectations.

Here is another example.

> YOU: You never hug me anymore. I barely get any affection from you at all. In fact, this morning when I was sad after that conversation with [a friend], I needed a hug from you. You knew that, and you all but avoided me.
>
> SPOUSE: I didn't know you needed a hug. If you wanted a hug, why didn't you just ask for one? What am I, a mind reader? I would have hugged you if you'd asked.
>
> YOU: I shouldn't *have* to ask. You should want to give me affection. Remember when we were dating? You could hardly keep your hands off me. Those days are sure gone! Now it's like pulling teeth to get you to hold my hand.

SPOUSE: See! When I don't hug you I get a lecture, and when I offer to hug you I get a lecture. I just can't please you no matter what I do. What's the use?

Should people who are married show support and have physical affection for each other? Of course. Again, this scenario is not only about affection. It is also about one spouse failing to live up to the expectations of the other. And mostly, it's about how people attempt to "fix" their inadequate false gods.

A second dynamic that can take place happens when you think your spouse's behavior is actually harmful in some way. This might range from mild insensitivity to gross immorality. No matter, this negative performance on their part makes them seem broken in your eyes. No one wants a *false god* that is broken. Therefore, you exert pressure on your spouse to change the negative behaviors into positives, or at least to hide them.

Dynamically, it looks like this:

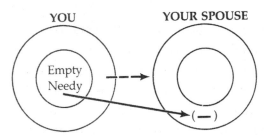

Your spouse's negative performance is represented by a minus sign (–). Again, the lines represent what you want, and the tactics you use to try to get what you want.

There is an abundance of verbal tactics used to change the other person's behavior. Here are some samples:

- Blaming: If you didn't do [such and such], we wouldn't be in such a mess.

- Comparing: Why can't you act like your [sibling, neighbor, friend]? You never see them doing that, do you?

- Challenging: If you really loved me, you wouldn't be
  _____ .

- Shaming: I can't believe you did that. What's wrong with you? What would the people at church think?

- Denial: If you're going to act that way, at least don't let [kids, parents, in-laws, friends] see you.

There are many other ways you can try to fix your spouse. Let me make it very clear that it is not okay, in my opinion, for people to act in ways that are mildly or grossly negative. And it is normal for those on the receiving end of negative behavior to be affected. What we are focusing on, however, is not the negative behaviors. We are focusing on the impulse to idolatry that causes us to try to draw our peace and well-being from something or someone other than Jesus Christ. Both husbands and wives struggle equally with "fixing" their broken false gods.

In some relationships, people even focus on someone's behavior to the point that they try to fix what is *not* broken. We've all seen examples of this. A husband will tell a story about what happened last Wednesday night, but the wife argues that the event happened on Tuesday night. The argument that follows lacks significance but not fervor. The same trivial "fixing" occurs when a heated discussion arises over which way the toilet paper roll should be mounted or where the toothpaste tube should be squeezed.

3. Fixing Yourself (to Fix the Other Person)

The third scenario that often occurs in a marriage is that a man or woman attempts to fix him/herself in the hope of changing his/her spouse. Very simply put, we sometimes tell ourselves: *If I get myself straightened out, then he/she will change.*

The primary example of this is the kind of false submission that is too often encouraged by many Christian pastors, teachers, and seminar leaders. We will consider the characteristics of true submission later. Too often we are taught to go along with something outwardly, while inwardly we strongly disagree. *This is not submission. It is pretending.*

John, for example, set his sights on buying a new little electric motor for his small fishing boat. Andrea wasn't really happy with John's idea. Early in their marriage, they'd had some loud arguments about money that made Andrea feel very uncomfortable, a feeling she really didn't like at all. She had learned, however, that a different tactic brought about the result she wanted: When John talked about the motor he wanted to buy, Andrea simply said nothing at all. It was not exactly that she gave John the silent treatment, but there was enough coolness that John read her silent message: *I don't want you to buy the motor. Go ahead and buy it if you want to, but I won't be happy if you do.* John and Andrea's pastor had recently taught about the husband's need to love and serve his wife and family. After picking up enough chilly signals, John thought about what his pastor had said, and decided that the best and most loving thing to do was to drop the idea of buying the motor for his fishing boat and not bring it up again. John hated it when Andrea went silent on him. It made him feel unmanly in some way.

Is this an example of submitting to your spouse in love? No. Andrea's silence was not submission. And John did not want to submit himself to the discomfort of honest dialogue, which might have led to true consensus. He wanted outward peace with Andrea at any price. With this approach, John would never come to understand Andrea's hopes or fears at a deep level, and never deal honestly with the resentment he came to feel whenever he felt his plans were stifled. This is not a one-flesh marriage; it is a win-lose relationship.

Sara-Lyn's difficulties with Bruce ran along similar lines. After two years of marriage, she found that most of the major responsibilities fell to her, including seeing that bills were paid on time, their cars were serviced regularly, and child-training matters were dealt with.

Bruce was a deacon in their church and led an adult Bible study, so most of their friends complimented him on what a wonderful, dedicated Christian husband and father he was— though nothing was further from the truth. When it came to his family, Bruce was actually quite irresponsible. He often forgot to pay bills because he preferred to spend his evenings glued to the television. Rather than taking a truly active role in guiding and training their three children, an angry shout was supposed to change their misbehavior.

When Sara-Lyn periodically wore herself out carrying all the weight Bruce refused to pick up, she would try to raise whatever issue was weighing her down the most. Bruce would explode and accuse her of being critical. If she persisted, pleading with him to take on more of the load, he would sometimes get so enraged that he slammed the wall with his fist—and then resorted to the one "knock-out punch" that always worked: "You're *pushing* me—and that proves what the *real* problem is here. You've got a controlling, rebellious spirit." Then he would quote and misquote Scriptures at her, until she was Bible-beaten into her place again.

When Sara-Lyn came to see me, it was little wonder she was on the verge of an emotional collapse. She had a washed-out, hopeless look in her eyes. She was sure that she was a terrible Christian because, try as she might to "submit" to Bruce, her heart kept telling her something was missing from his concept of what a Christian marriage should be. Her submission was not from the heart or the spirit—it was a knuckling under, a fear of Bruce's uncontrolled, childish anger. Their pastor was commending Bruce for keeping his home in order, based on the superficial signs he saw in public. Sara-Lyn was seeing things as they really were, and suffering with the sad discrepancy. This, as I say, is not submission; it is keeping peace merely to avoid a "spiritual wife-beating."

When anyone "submits" outwardly in order to escape fear, ease guilt, or "prove" their spirituality, there is no real submission. True submission releases us from fear, helps us face and change behaviors that make us guilty, and causes us to grow stronger in spirit. Accept no substitutes.

THE SERIOUS MATTER OF FALSE SUBMISSION

Because false submission is such a widespread problem, eroding otherwise good Christian marriages, I want to address it in a little more detail. Let's examine it by walking through another real-life counseling situation.

Not long ago, a couple came to me for counseling. Their relationship hadn't worked for five and a half of the six years they had been married. The wife, Chris, recited incident after incident of how Carl made decisions regardless of what she thought. For a long time she had pretended to agree, thinking this would soften his heart. (Notice the attempt at "fixing" going on here.) Carl wasn't changing, though, and Chris felt she had lost her own integrity as well. If she ever hinted that she didn't like his decision, Carl began to complain mercilessly about her to everyone, until she was simply worn out. Now she harbored resentment that was deeply embedded, and it was beginning to spill into other areas of their relationship.

After almost twenty minutes of listening to Chris's explanation, Carl folded his arms across his chest and asked me, "What do you think it means when the Bible says that the wife is supposed to be *subject* to the husband?" (Further on, I'll tell you what I told Carl.)

My purpose now is to cement this concept in your mind: Chris, like a lot of other Christian wives, really did care about doing what the Scriptures said. But because of the power manipulations of

60

this very *un*Christlike husband, she fell into the trap of playing a "peace-at-any-price" game.

Need I repeat? This is not submission; nor is it spiritual husbandry in the humility of Christ. Simply put, if you've got to demand or force submission, or pretend it, you do not know what it is.

CONCLUSION: THIS DOESN'T WORK

The reason these various "try-hard" solutions can't possibly work is that no man or woman is powerful enough to provide life and value to their spouse. Spouses weren't created by God to "fix" spouses. Jesus came to provide life and value to each one of us.

Isn't this all rather theological sounding? Yes it is, but it leads to the reasons why, on a very practical level, the relationships I have described simply cannot work: A relationship in which performance is demanded or expected is a *no-win* situation for both parties.

Can you think of a time when you knew that the only reason someone did a certain thing for you was because you pressured them until they gave in? Didn't it seem empty? Or perhaps you are the one who gives in under pressure. In either case, the action is just a form of pacification, a compromise at best.

When a relationship devolves into a win-lose exercise, it will eventually wear out. Love will evaporate, and hearts and minds will turn to various forms of escape. This is a serious matter—whether the marriage remains outwardly intact or ends in divorce—and it is the topic of the next chapter.

DISCUSSION QUESTIONS

1. *Why is it important to listen to someone's pain and need instead of giving a pat answer like "Just pray about it" or "Snap out of it"?*

2. *Is it common in married couples to live in denial that there are problems in the marriage? If yes, why do you think this is true?*

3. *Does it ever work to try to "fix" your spouse? Have you ever tried to do this? How did that work for you?*

4. *How can a spouse become a false god?*

5. *Submission as taught in Scripture is often grossly misunderstood by the church. Give some examples of false submission and some examples of biblical submission.*

5. Trying to Escape the Curse

What does the word *marriage* mean to you?

A marriage is not just a contract signed by two people. It is not an arrangement. A marriage is not the result of one moment when two people get all dressed up and make promises to each other in front of a crowd.

Marriage, in the true sense, is a living entity—and sometimes living entities begin to lose strength because they have not been properly nourished.

Couples decide they need marriage counseling for a variety of reasons. I employ many different tactics in order to help them. The individuals in the marriage gain different insights into their marital problems. But one thing remains constant in every session, and that is my stance toward the relationship: *This marriage can be revived.*

Nevertheless, some people leave relationships because they sense it is the only way they can survive. Most of these people have exhausted themselves with inadequate self-effort and in doing so have ensured the hopelessness of the situation.

WHEN A SPOUSE LEAVES

Sometimes it becomes apparent that none of the solutions mentioned in the last chapter are going to fix the marriage relationship. Some people then choose a fourth alternative: They decide to leave. For some the "leaving" amounts to emotional abandonment, while others actually pack their bags and walk out. The fact of the matter is, a person can walk out on a marriage and never find what they were looking for in that relationship. We Christians condemn divorce, but my purpose here is to look at what happens inwardly *before* and *after* divorce occurs.

THE "HEART" OF A DIVORCE

Imagine that a day finally comes when you have tried everything, and trying hard has failed. Your efforts to deny the problem no longer mask the gulf that exists between you and your mate. Both you and your spouse feel totally exhausted as a result of your unsuccessful attempts to "fix" each other. You decide to separate or get a divorce.

When this happens, the relationship is only being made to appear as broken and unhealthy as it has been in reality. The fact is, somewhere along the way the relationship died, and you have failed to revive it through the power of your own self-effort.

As a result, you can accept another message inwardly: *Shame on you!* In fact, shame—the sense of defectiveness you've been trying the entire time to soothe—is actually the invisible specter that's been driving you all along. You have not only carried a sense of shame, now there is "proof" you are inadequate, and your friends are about to reinforce the dreaded message. To those looking on, the breakup is quite a shock. To them, you looked fine outwardly. Their responses vary:

"How could this have happened? He was in the ministry!"

"Wasn't she the head of her church's women's ministry?"

"Didn't he talk at one time about going to the mission field?"

"I can't remember a time when they weren't together."

The responses document the fact that too often it is more important for a Christian couple to *appear* as if they have a healthy marriage than to actually have one—which requires disagreement, work, and real one-flesh unity in which both parties grow healthier.

"IF WE DON'T FILE, GOD WON'T KNOW"

I am convinced that God hates divorce and the damage it causes. I am also convinced that He hates every bit as much the shaming, broken-down marriages that masquerade as Christian marriages because of the spiritual damage they cause in the life of one or both partners, not to mention the children.

I have noticed in Christian marriages two curious and disturbing phenomena. First, many Christians think that God likes curse-full marriages better than divorce: In other words, a hurtful, unhealthy marriage is more pleasing to God than a divorce. Second, many of them also think that as long as they don't get a piece of paper certifying their broken relationship, God can't tell that it's broken. Too many people remain in unhealthy marriages that have *none* of what God says is important in marriage. Yet the reason they don't get divorced is because the Bible is against it. And they say, "We just want to do what would be pleasing to God." So they remain in a disconnected, hurtful marriage for six months, a year, ten years—maybe even fifty years. Then they pat themselves on the back for caring about what God says about marriage, when there is no evidence in their marriage of what God truly wants. And all along, they thought God didn't see the truth because they never got a piece of paper from the government.

This is a disturbing statement, I know—but for too many Christians, being married has come to mean *not being divorced*. They think that as long as they have a piece of paper that says their marriage is intact, God won't notice that it's broken. It is as though God cares about the letter of the law so much that He isn't able to notice the true spirit of a marriage.

Miserable marriages and divorce are both wrong; both are unhealthy alternatives. It seems that many Christians are willing to settle for a sickly imitation of the real thing. Is a lousy marriage better than divorce? I believe God grieves over both.

SIMULTANEOUSLY STAYING AND LEAVING

There is a dilemma for those people who prefer curse-full marriages to divorce, and who are trying to impress God by adhering to the letter of the law. Since they need to outwardly perform in accordance with the written Word in order to keep their sense of God's approval, they must find a way to stay in the relationship. But when the relationship has become painful, a constant indictment against them, a reminder of shame, and a drain on their energy, they look for a way to leave. Choosing to stay *and* leave is perhaps the most tiring alternative of all. Let me explain.

Lee realizes she is incapable of changing Jerry, that he will never live up to her expectations. Lee also realizes she is incapable of changing herself enough to live up to Jerry's loudly voiced expectations of her. The relationship has become one of constant reminders of emptiness, inadequacy, and shame. Because they are Christians, Lee and Jerry are determined never to divorce.

Lee is also a business consultant. She is highly respected in the workplace, in constant demand, and is paid a great deal of money for her time. Lee is constantly affirmed by her clients, and is rewarded with checks and bonuses—tangible reminders that she is capable and competent. At home, however, she is constantly reminded how inadequate and incompetent she is as a spouse.

Frankly, it is simply easier and less painful for a person to spend eight to ten hours every weekday in an environment where he/she is being affirmed. Then the relationship looks like this, as one party looks outside the relationship for fulfillment:

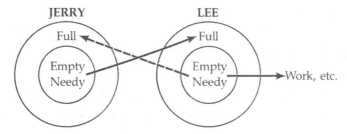

In this case, the broken line represents Lee's choice to give up on her former source of value, which was Jerry's performance. Now she is drawing her sense of worth from her work.

ACCEPTABLE FORMS OF ADULTERY

In truth, Lee is being adulterous in her relationship with Jerry. She is doing this through a relationship with work that amounts to a socially acceptable form of marital unfaithfulness. Let me hasten to clarify: Every woman who works is not committing "spiritual adultery" or robbing her husband and family. Men can be just as prone, and perhaps more prone, to vanish into their work as a means of avoiding problems at home and getting the ego-affirmation that is only a false substitute for having real life and worth as a result of Christ within. It's "the American Way."

There are many ways in which people commit marital unfaithfulness that is not in the form of sexual adultery. Some people vanish into TV watching or Internet surfing: For some people it is a much less painful alternative than trying to have a relationship in which you never feel good enough. Some people vanish into making money: For them, having a big bank account serves as tangible (and false) evidence of their personal value, and it salves the pain of a not-good-enough marriage. I have counseled with clients whose third marriage is on the rocks, and who make a lot of money. And when their marriage one day collapses, they are totally surprised. After all, they're so immersed in business, and successful too—why can't they make a go of it as a marriage partner?

THE STORY OF MIKE AND DORA

The many struggles of Mike and Dora, early in their marriage, gives another view of this dynamic. It also serves as a reminder that the staying/leaving "solution" can develop over things much less significant than money or work.

Mike grew up in a rural area of upper Michigan. Through his childhood, several lessons were deeply ingrained in him by his father. One was a love for hunting and fishing, and many other activities that had to do with the outdoors. In the fall, almost every day after school, Mike went hunting alone or with his dad. In the spring it was fishing. Experiences in the outdoors provided refreshment, and even a perspective on God's creative genius. Yes, there were many healthy and positive aspects to all this outdoor activity, but it was also one of the ways Mike's dad avoided facing the stressful aspects of his life. Subtly, it was communicated to Mike: When the going gets tough, men go fishing.

Another lesson imparted to Mike was that it was his job to make sure everyone else was happy. His father contributed to this with outbursts of anger for which he never took responsibility. It was then Mike's job, or the job of another family member, to prevent the rage, and it was their fault when it happened.

On the surface, Dora's family situation looked much more caring than Mike's, and it was not nearly as volatile. Nevertheless, she grew up with a father who communicated that he was not all that interested in her. Not that he stated his disinterest—but by remaining passive and uninvolved he neglected to communicate love and acceptance. For her part, Dora's mom acted as if men were more important than women, and made it her job to see that Dora's dad was content—even if it meant that she herself didn't have a life. Dora learned to interpret absence as non-acceptance and leaving as abandonment. She also learned that what men thought or wanted was the most important thing.

So in one form or another both Dora and Mike came into their marriage with a rule that said: "Good, valuable, acceptable, spiritual spouses meet all the needs of their spouse." Their relationship consisted of a lot of effort trying to live up to their own expectations as well as those of their partner. This was also true when it came to fishing. Consider the following dialogue, representative of what it sounded like when Mike wanted to go fishing, with my parenthetical comments:

MIKE: I'm planning to go fishing next weekend.

DORA: Again? You're always going fishing. (This was not true.)

MIKE: That's not true! I hardly ever get to go fishing. (This was not true either.) Besides, I'm going with one of the kids from the junior-high youth group and his dad. (Who can argue with ministry?)

DORA: You'd rather be with them than with me.

MIKE: That's not true. (Although this scene had been repeated over and over again, it was a toss-up.) It's just that I really like to go fishing.

Let's examine this scene a bit: Fishing did restorative things for Mike that Dora couldn't do and didn't have to do. But Dora believed that good Christian husbands and wives meet all the needs of their spouses. Therefore, she interpreted Mike's love of fishing as a lack of love for her. She also felt indicted as a wife because, after all, if she was being the kind of wife she was supposed to be, Mike wouldn't even want to go fishing; all his needs would be met at home.

For his part, Mike felt guilty when he went fishing because he knew how sad Dora was. If he stayed home, he felt sad and angry because he really wanted to be out there in that rowboat. He also knew that Dora still wouldn't be satisfied and would want him to stay home the next time as well. And if Mike did choose to stay home, Dora felt guilty! There was no way for either of them to win. So Mike thought, *If both of us are going to feel lousy either way, I might as well go fishing.*

Should one person in a relationship constantly be off fishing (or watching TV, or whatever else) instead of being with his/her spouse? Absolutely not. Should one person in a relationship be upset any time his/her spouse pursues a pastime that is important to them? No. What I have described, however, is not simply an issue of fishing vs. staying home. It is not about the outward activities at all. It is about Dora placing expectations on Mike and on herself that neither of them can fill. Mike's method of handling the problem was to run. Dora's was to hold on more tightly. Neither would face the matter of wrong expectations. This kind of dynamic sucks the life out of any relationship.

Wrong expectations showed themselves in other ways in this relationship. Dora sometimes felt sad and would try to tell Mike. Mike thought that a good Christian husband should always know what to say to help his wife not be so sad. So he would launch into a big lecture in an attempt to fix Dora's sadness. Instead of feeling supported, she felt even more sad and controlled as well. When Mike realized his talk didn't work, he'd get frustrated. Upon seeing Mike's frustration, Dora would decide not to tell him when she was sad in order to control his frustration. Eventually, when Dora shared her sadness, Mike would not say anything. Wanting some kind of response, Dora would insinuate that "good husbands know what to do," and Mike would feel as though he couldn't win either way. No one felt affirmed. No one felt affirming. In fact, this downward spiral resulted in much tiredness for both of them.

AN UNACCEPTABLE FORM OF ADULTERY

Leaving a relationship could also take the form of an extramarital affair. If a man or woman chooses to have an affair, there are several things to take into account. First, no one gravitates toward an empty-looking spouse substitute. Therefore, this new love interest will have to look *full* on the outside. "Full" simply means having characteristics and behaviors different than the spouse left behind. Second, a person who leaves is still under the illusion that people can fill people. They have simply chosen to exchange one false god, who has not been able to fill them, for another that promises to. If a Christian realizes they are on the brink of adultery and turns to a counselor for help, they too often receive counsel that they should simply try harder in their marriage. But if the inner, spiritual patterns of idolatry are not addressed, the couple is destined to clone those patterns in future relationships, whether in this marriage, or their second—or third.

THE MOST ACCEPTABLE FORM OF ADULTERY

As we have seen, an affair is adultery in its most unacceptable form. And work-related absence from a spouse can become a type of adultery in a more acceptable form. But I have witnessed the sad effects of an even more acceptable form of marital unfaithfulness. This is when ministry involvement serves the purpose of keeping a couple from facing painful relationship issues. This is often very difficult to confront because a busy ministry can masquerade as holiness and commitment to God.

Paul leads a Bible study where he receives constant affirmation for his insight and wisdom. He visits people in the hospital who are always grateful for the visit and who boast to others about his generous concern. Many in his church praise him for the selfless sacrifice of family time in service of others. Sherry, his wife, feels otherwise. But how can she object without feeling enormously guilty? God is pleased with Paul because he is so active in ministry, right? And it is easy for Paul to avoid Sherry's indicting comments at home for the positive compliments he receives while doing ministry.

Those who try to confront this are often accused of being unspiritual or not caring about what God wants. Countless wives of Bible college or seminary students find their way to counselors because they feel as if they are losing their marriage relationship as a result of the ministry or preparation for it. When they raise questions at home, they are put down by their husband, the professor, the pastor, or even the president of the college for "not caring about the work of the kingdom."

In truth, these women are often trying to confront a religiously acceptable form of adultery.

THE MOST DAMAGING IDOLATRY OF ALL

I have mentioned several manifestations of adultery. They all result from idolatry—that is by trying to get needs met from human resources instead of from God, who is the Source. There is one form of idolatry, however, that is the most damaging of all. It results in a last-ditch effort on the part of a couple to acquire a sense of value and meaning. One day they look at their little "empty" newborn and begin to rely on the performance of that child as their source of value and meaning. Dynamically, it looks like this:

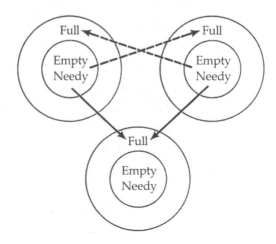

In this scenario, the children are made to feel that their reason for being is to fill and fulfill Mom and Dad—a job that is not theirs, and a job at which they can only fail. And now, more than a marriage relationship has been affected and infected. The curse has been passed to another generation.

Tired marriage partners are not the only products of curse-full relationships. In the next chapter we will examine curse-full parenting, and the tired children who result.

DISCUSSION QUESTIONS

1. *Marriage is more than a contract between two people. What is a good definition of marriage?*

2. *The Bible says God hates divorce. But if a couple stays in a miserable marriage merely to avoid divorce, do you think God is pleased? Explain your answer and discuss.*

3. *What are some "acceptable" forms of adultery?*

4. *An affair is the most obvious form of adultery. What is the "most acceptable" form of adultery? Why does this form seem acceptable?*

5. *How can children enter into the dynamics of adults trying to find fulfillment in their lives?*

6. Recycling the Curse

When our girls were first born, Holly and I would drop what we were doing at the sound of the smallest squeak. A tiny whimper could get us up in the middle of the night from a deep sleep. (Honesty compels me to say that *Holly* was the one who got up most.) We learned quickly: Babies are the ultimate takers. They scream, wave their arms, kick their feet, and people bring them things and do things for them. That is as it should be for that stage of their lives.

But little babies gradually turn into adolescents, and then into eighteen-year-old adults. If they are still screaming and waving their arms so people will give them attention, then something has gone wrong between infancy and adulthood. And if they become dads and moms, and their family members have to tiptoe around to avoid their screaming fits, something has gone wrong between infancy and parenthood.

In a healthy family, parents understand that they are to provide an environment and relationships in which the children's needs are met. They remind children that Jesus is their Source of life, value,

and meaning. Rules are in place to protect the children and provide a structure in which to learn. In a curse-full family, children
are expected to meet the needs of the parents. Rules are in place to
control and fix. In this dynamic, when the kids are fixed, the parents
feel good about themselves.

IT'S OKAY TO BE NEEDY

To understand the damaging effects that curse-full families
inflict upon children, we must pick up where the last chapter left off.
We saw that, at times, parents try to fill their own empty neediness
by drawing upon the good performance of their child.

Little babies don't know they are loved and accepted; they have
to learn that. They don't know they have worth; they have to experience that. They are not capable; they need a safe place in which to
practice living. And they don't know that they are not alone. Without
your presence, they feel alone. *They are needy.*

These needy little people are also vulnerable. They can become
victims to the hostile forces around them. They can be controlled. So
these little ones must enter a process in which they develop a strong
sense of who they are. They need to grow deep in strength, wisdom,
and a sense of fullness so they are no longer so vulnerable. But curse-
full families don't care about wisdom, fullness, and identity. They care
about external performance. Strength is defined in terms of positive
performance. Health is seen in behavioral terms. Whether or not God
loves you is dependent on how well you obey on any given day.

ACTING HEALTHY

In controlling, shaming families, love and acceptance come as
a reward for jumping through certain behavioral hoops. People are
validated for their *right doing*, not simply for *being*. Children grow

up needy and empty. To earn personal approval, which they never really receive, they learn to perform well. Good behavior is whatever the people with power in the family decide is positive. Hence, adults may be lulled into believing that their children are spiritually strong and mature, when in fact they may be people pleasers.

Periodically, I am asked to speak in a public-school setting on the topic of drug and alcohol abuse. One statement that always triggers controversy is this: "Just because you have somehow gotten your child to stop using chemicals, and instead they are now playing football or are in band, does not necessarily mean you have a healthy child." Parents flip. They're shocked, indignant, confused. To some people it has never occurred to them that an unhealthy person could act in a positive way if the payoff looked good. Nice, positive behavior is automatically equated with health.

Ask any counselor how many "nice" Christian people show up, dying inside.

VULNERABLE PEOPLE GET SQUEEZED

I'd like to do an experiment. We'll start with a person who is healthy-looking on the outside but empty and vulnerable on the inside. Let's see what happens when we strip them of their full-looking exterior and place them in different environments. Let's call this guy David. The first environment in which we'll place David will be with a negative peer group. (To the religious system in which I grew up, this group would have been called "the world.")

NEGATIVE PEER GROUP

Empty
Needy

The arrows coming from the outside represent the negative peer pressure placed upon David to act in a way that is acceptable to the group (e.g., use drugs, sleep around, vandalize, shoplift, cheat in school, and lie to his parents).

Along with each expected performance comes the offer (verbal or nonverbal) of acceptance: "If you do it our way, we'll accept you." And, there is the promise of importance: "This will really make you a man/woman." A chance to belong: "You are really out of it. Come join our group. You don't have to be alone."

If David believes that doing these negative things—thereby earning the approval of the crowd—will make him OK, he may decide to do the negative behaviors. The empty neediness has not really been taken care of. David has just been squeezed to look like the environment around him. That would make him look like this:

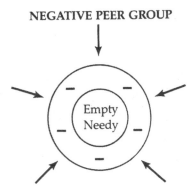

Please be clear on this: Even though David has chosen to act in negative ways, he is still empty on the inside and full on the outside. Negative behaviors look right in a negative crowd. But emptiness is still empty in any crowd.

CONTROLLING BY THE CURSE-FULL FAMILY

I have just described a young man who is empty on the inside *and* empty on the outside. This child drives his parents, grandparents, pastors, and teachers nuts: The more behavior-oriented they are, the crazier he makes them. David's lack of positive behaviors and abundance of negative behaviors is bad public relations for those who equate behavior with health. "What would people think?" "Where did we go wrong?" "It's not our fault—it's those friends he's been hanging out with!" "How can he do this to us?" "What can we do to stop this?"

At this point, the curse-full family may do what it does best— that is, they may try to control David's behavior by exerting some pressure of their own. One more negative behavior (depicted as a minus sign in the diagram) and there will be consequences:

- Skip one more homework assignment and you're off the football team.
- One more incident and we're sending you to a Christian school.
- Keep doing that and God will punish you.

Actually, if David keeps following the wrong crowd, he may get into enough trouble and experience enough pain for him to decide to quit behaving negatively. Or maybe one day he will notice that he still doesn't feel loved, accepted, or capable. He is just as alone as he was before he followed the crowd. In fact, he is really the same young man as when our story began: an empty, vulnerable person.

CHRISTIAN "BEHAVIOR MODIFICATION"

So many people view the church or Christian family as simply an environment whose purpose is to exert positive peer pressure. This is simply behavior modification in a religious context. To see the best this has to offer, let's continue to follow David as he makes the turnaround his Christian family has been praying for. David joins the church youth group, still looking for love and acceptance.

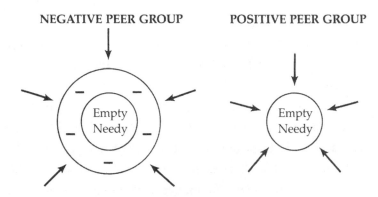

The arrows coming toward David from the outside now represent peer pressure placed upon him to act in a positive way. "Don't listen to the world's music, listen to our music." "Don't read their books, read ours." "Don't talk like they talk, talk like we do." "Don't dress like they do, dress like us." "Don't go where they go, go with us." Once again, if he fulfills the performance expectations, there is the promise of love, the sense of worth, and the security of receiving acceptance from the group.

If David believes that doing these new positive behaviors has the power to meet his needs inside, he will go along with the new regimen. Nothing is really different about David, though. He has simply decided to please a different crowd. Once again, he has been squeezed from the outside, and so he looks on the outside like the environment around him. Now he looks like this:

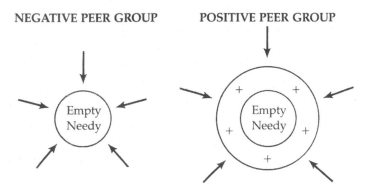

David has chosen to act in a positive manner. He is full on the outside but still empty on the inside. And while positive behaviors are defined as full by the positive crowd, emptiness is still empty in any crowd.

Sure, David pleases the socks off his parents, grandparents, teachers, and pastor. The more performance-oriented they are, the more pleased. His positive performance *earns* their approval— though they would be shocked to think of it in that way. And they might back off, because it is no longer necessary for them to exert so much control. In effect, David is left in control of everyone's happiness and peace again.

WHERE IS GOD?

Ironically, the Christian family that is operating under the performance curse will even give God credit for all of this. "Praise the Lord!" they say. "What a fine work the Lord is doing in David's life." But does David's change really have anything to do with the inner transforming work of the Holy Spirit? Or has David simply been squeezed into a prettier-looking version of emptiness?

If David keeps acting this way, and if he is continually affirmed for his positive exterior, then the qualities that constitute inside fullness might be neglected. He could one day come to the end of his self-effort resources and have nothing on the inside on which to draw. Or, worse yet, he might *never* come to the end of his resources, in which case inside questions of the heart and how it is separated unto God for His use might never be addressed.

A FINAL LOOK AT DAVID

What are the results of our experiment? On the one hand, David used to look like this:

He was empty on the outside because of his behavior choices; he was empty and tired on the inside because no amount of negative behavior on the outside can meet inside needs. He was "bad publicity" for his family and church and easy to spot as an unhealthy person.

On the other hand, David now looks like this:

He is full on the outside because of his behavior choices; he is empty and tired on the inside because no amount of positive behavior on the outside can meet inside needs. He is "good publicity" for his family and church and hard to spot as an unhealthy person.

I have just one question: Which version of David would you say is healthier? Let me help you out, from the viewpoint of a counselor. People become unhealthy when their outside fails to match their inside. Consequently, health means learning to live consistently on the outside with what is on the inside. Therefore, if your definition of health includes integrity, maturity, responsibility, respect, and spiritual depth, you will conclude that neither version of David is healthy. It's just that one looks better than the other.

Which version of David will be more tired in the long run? My opinion is that the "good" David—the one who is empty on the inside and full on the outside—will be more tired. Why? Because it's a lot of work to always give the right answer and seldom the true one. Even if you are a mess on the inside, you must say you're "fine." If you hate someone, you have to say you love them in Christian love.

I don't know of any parent who would say that their goal in parenting is to produce people who are empty on the inside and empty on the outside. It cannot be our goal as Christian parents to raise children to adulthood who are still empty but who have learned to look and act more acceptably than the world's various versions of acceptability. *We can do better than that.*

In part 2 of this book, which follows, we will examine the means by which you create a healthy relationship context between spouses and between parents and children, so that full behavior comes as an expression of fullness on the inside. We will begin to see how you can make your family one in which grace is in place.

DISCUSSION QUESTIONS

1. *Where does a person's value come from? Can it ever be earned?*

2. *Explain how responding to peer pressure can still leave a person empty on the inside.*

3. *What is the danger of positive peer pressure versus negative peer pressure?*

4. *Has this chapter helped you to think about what constitutes a true Christian versus someone who looks and acts like one? Explain.*

PART II

Families "by the Book"

Introduction

It doesn't take a social scientist to figure out that families today are in trouble. Adultery, divorce, depression, rebellion, teen suicide, alcoholism, workaholism, and a host of other "isms" have reached epidemic proportions. Benjamin Franklin is thought to have said, "A disease is never brought under control simply by treating the casualties." Wouldn't it be great if we could prevent some of these spiritual diseases from claiming casualties in our families?

Is it possible to build a healthy family from the inside-out and prevent such devastating problems? Can we create family dynamics that break with the patterns that perpetuate hurt and sin? I believe the answer to these questions is *yes!*

It is not my intention, however, to offer the next and latest formula for having a Christian family. This section is not mainly about "how-to's." It is about hearts; it is about our opportunity to examine the state-of-heart with which we approach the task of building healthy family relationships.

I am referring to this section as Families "by the Book" because the principles it contains come right out of Scripture. They are offered as a strong structure to be placed under the everyday work you do—the spiritual support-system, if you will, that can help you devise your own "how-to's" as you build grace and empowerment into your own family. Yes, I will illustrate the principles with some personal experiences. But my prayer is that, as you read, the Holy Spirit will bring to light ways that you can apply what you learn. For that is, in fact, at the very core of what I'm suggesting: As you become rightly related to God, by His grace, He will lead you in modeling the spiritual life, and in training your children how to live happy, free, fruitful lives.

7. A Real Marriage

In chapter 4, I mentioned a man who, in a counseling session, wanted to know what I thought Paul meant in Ephesians 5, when he instructed wives to submit to their husbands. It was quite apparent that he wanted me to say something that would support the spirit in which he used this verse—which was to maintain the upper hand. He employed many methods to accomplish this: Sometimes he yelled at his wife. Other times he whined and pouted. At times he would not talk to his wife for days, just to punish her for not giving him his way. This time he was using the Bible.

In a marriage counseling setting, I find it painful and frustrating to see one party using the Bible to try to drive someone. It is more frustrating when they try to get me to help. This man wanted to place himself over his wife by invoking Scripture, and he was also trying to borrow authority from me: If I agreed with him, he would have "won" again.

Actually, this is a very common occurrence. When I see a couple in marriage counseling, it is typical for the husband to know more about the "wife verses" than the "husband verses," and vice versa. Each party uses a variety of methods and spends all kinds of energy trying to get the other person to obey their verse (and hardly any energy worrying about their own). This is the curse in operation.

Our job, however, as Christian spouses, is not to drive each other to perform well but rather to learn God's plan. In this chapter we will focus on what Scripture has to say about God's plan for marriage.

MARRIAGE, AND GOD'S TRUE PLAN

Ephesians 5, verses 22–33, seems to be the most referred to, most quoted passage by those trying to understand God's plan for marriage. But it is necessary to include verses 18–21 in order to get at the heart of God's marriage plan. For a long time these seemed like disconnected passages. Verses 18–21 seemed so spiritual, because they are about being filled with the Spirit. It seemed that Paul abruptly began an entirely different teaching with verse 22.

Not long after starting to counsel couples, I saw the connection. Paul began the teaching on family relationships with the command to "be filled with the Spirit." And the reason he did so is because of how deeply the curse has infiltrated husband-wife, parent-child relationships. In counseling, I see husbands who have tried to get filled from their wives, wives who have tried to get filled from their husbands, and even parents who have tried to get filled from their children. Again, this is the curse in operation.

Paul is reminding Christians to turn to the Holy Spirit as their Source of filling. He is telling them where their filling is to come from—and that is from God.

Therefore, I have come to believe it is essential to understand

Ephesians 5:18–21 in order to have the correct lens through which to view the teaching on Christian relationships.

DRUNK WITH THE SPIRIT?

Paul says, "And do not get drunk with wine, for that is dissipation, but be filled with the Spirit" (Ephesians 5:18). The contrast between drunk and filled is significant. Let's consider what Paul is *not* saying. "Filled," here, is not a word denoting quantity; Paul is not talking about how much of the Spirit we have. He is not saying, "You are only half full (like a glass of water), and you need to be completely filled." Romans 8:9 indicates that if you belong to Jesus, you have the *entire* Holy Spirit dwelling in you. Neither is Paul saying, "Remember how you used to get drunk with wine? Well, now, instead of getting drunk with wine, get drunk with the Spirit."

Unfortunately, there are Christians who do this. They are so "*Spirit*-filled" that they are like those who are drunk. They don't see, hear, feel, or enter into the pain and struggles of others. They are numb. "Filled with the Spirit" results in new eyes that see more, new ears that hear more, a new heart that cares more, and a new Source through which we have power to enter into the pain of others and make a difference.

FILLED WITH THE SPIRIT!

"Filled" is the Greek word *pleroma*, which has a couple of meanings that apply here. First, it could mean *permeated*. Permeated is what happens to a glass of water when you drop an Alka-Seltzer into it. It becomes permeated. There is no part of the glass of water that doesn't have Alka-Seltzer in it.

Pleroma is also the word that would be used to describe a sail when it is full of wind. A filled sail is what empowers or propels a sailboat. (Now, this is where what I learned in high-school physics comes in handy.) It is not the wind in the sail that propels the boat—the boat is not pressured forward from behind. In fact, the wind creates a negative pressure—a vacuum—in front of the sail. This vacuum is the force that attracts the boat forward. So being filled with the Spirit does not mean being power-driven through the Christian life, as if the Holy Spirit were a locomotive-wind behind us. Rather, it means being drawn into godly living by the Holy Spirit, who is in front of us, focusing us on God. I guess God knows about physics too.

We can learn even more about the meaning of a word by looking at its Greek form. In the case of "be filled . . ." it is in the present, passive, imperative form. Each of those aspects simply enrich the meaning.

An imperative is a command. The one commanding assumes that you have the power to carry through in your own power. But this command is given in a passive voice, which means it is not something you can do, but something that must be done to you or for you. Paul did not write, "Get (yourself) filled," or, "Fill yourself," which is an *active* imperative. Instead he wrote, "Allow yourself to be filled," which is a *passive* imperative. The easiest way to understand the present tense is to simply think of the phrase "whenever it is now." Thus, one literal rendering of "be filled with the Spirit" is this: "Allow yourself to be continuously filled with the Spirit." It is not something you *should*, or even *can* do. It is something you should and can *allow to be done to you*, whenever it is now. I have heard many people say things like, "My [wife/husband/child/pastor] is a Spirit-filled believer." In light of what we have just learned, there is no such thing as a Spirit-filled believer. If we remain true to God's Word, it is accurate to say that there are simply believers who are allowing themselves to be continuously filled now . . . and now . . . and now. . . .

Therefore, it seems that Paul is instructing Christians to enter the fight that is the essence of the Christian life: "Get your life from God. Remain in a continuously dependent relationship with Him in order to meet your needs. Do it! In fact, if Adam and Eve had remembered to do this, we wouldn't be having this little talk right now."

REVERSING THE CURSE

When we depend on God to meet our needs, it sends ripples through every relationship we have: "Speaking to one another in psalms and hymns and spiritual songs, singing and making melody with your heart to the Lord; always giving thanks for all things in the name of our Lord Jesus Christ to God, even the Father; and be subject to one another in the fear of Christ" (vv. 19–21).

What is extremely noteworthy here is that "speaking to one another," "singing and making melody," "giving thanks," and "being subject" are not imperatives. Paul is not saying, "Speak more kindly to each other, get a song in your heart, be more thankful to God, and be subject to one another!" The only imperative in this text is, "Be filled with the Spirit." All of these other things are what result when we allow ourselves to be filled by God. Even the "be subject to one another" is best read in the original language as the result of this filling from God.

The ramifications of being filled with the Spirit literally reverse the effects that the curse has on relationships. Let's look again at the diagram of curse-full relationships:

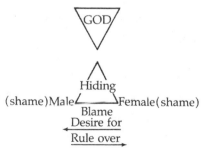

Look at the difference "being filled with the Spirit" makes in our relationships:

	THE CURSE	THE PLAN
With Others	blaming "desire for" (female toward male) "rule over" (male toward female)	psalms and hymns and spiritual songs (v. 19) subject to one another (v. 21)
Inside Ourselves	shame	a song in our hearts (v. 19)
With God	fear and hiding from God	going toward God with thanksgiving (vv. 19-20)

Here, for the sake of our understanding of marriage, I want to pay special attention to the phrase "be subject to one another." The word translated *"being subject"* is the Greek word *hupotasso*. It means "to arrange yourself underneath." It is a strong word having military overtones, as an infantry person would submit to the command of a general. As we've seen, "being subject" is a result.

And what a result! Remember the dynamics of the curse, as described in Genesis 3:16. Two people wind up locked in a power struggle. Both are over the other and both are under the other, because both are trying to rule. What Paul tells us in Ephesians is how to reverse and escape the curse.

BEING "SUBJECT"

Now we can talk, in context, about Paul's instruction, "Wives, be subject to your own husbands, as to the Lord." In some versions of the Bible, the words "be subject" are in italics; this indicates they are not found in the original Greek. They are implied. Therefore, verse 22 literally says, "Wives to your own husbands, as to the Lord." The concept "be subject" is borrowed from the verse before, which tells all Christians to "be subject to one another" as a result of being filled with the Spirit. A literal reading of verses 21 and 22, then, would be, "being subject to [arranging yourselves underneath] one another in reverence to Christ, wives to your own husbands. . . ."

In this passage of Ephesians, then, Paul is actually presenting a major concept that empowers us to live the Christian life, and then illustrating how it works within several kinds of relationships: wife/husband (5:22, 23); parent/child (6:1–4); and slave/master (6:5–9). In every instance he talks about what it means for two people to place themselves *under one another*. The conversation about submission only begins with wives in v. 22. So we cannot ignore what Paul has to say about husbands. If husbands are not to be submissive to their wives too, then there is no "being subject to one another."

Paul tells us, "For the husband is the head of the wife, as Christ also is the head of the church, He himself being the Savior of the body" (5:23). In other words, if you want to see and understand just what it means that the husband is the head of the wife, you need to understand what it means that Christ is the head of the church.

There are several places in Ephesians that shed light on this. In Ephesians 1:18–23 we see a picture of the powerful, eternal, already-victorious Christ whose headship over all things is a gift to the church. In Ephesians 4:7–16, we see an incredible picture of Christ's headship. It brings about our freedom and results in our enemy being defeated and taken captive. It is the reason why we have the gifts we need to learn, to grow, and to help others. In other words, the result of having Christ as our head is that we have everything we need to become and to do everything God plans for us. And the quintessential expression of spiritual headship was this: He sacrificed of His own physical, earthly life. This is underscored in 5:25, where Christ's love is expressed toward the church in that "he gave himself for her."

If Christ is over you and me (the church), it is not because He placed himself *over* us. It is because we placed ourselves *under* Him. In fact, bending your knee to Christ as Lord is how you become a Christian. We submit to His headship. But as you can see from the text, all the activity of Christ, who is our head, is to come under, to serve, to build, and even to die for the church. And the husband is the head of the wife, as Christ is the head of the church! So, husbands, if you are reminding your wife that you are the boss, then you are *not* the head of your wife as Christ is the head of the church.

In writing about the sad and widespread problem of spiritual abuse,[1] Dave Johnson and I explored what happens when leaders in the kingdom of God use worldly techniques to gain control and power. In this world, *leader* means *boss*, the one in charge, the one in front. But Jesus says that leaders are servants. (See Matthew 23:11; Luke 22:26.) It is the same way with the word *head*. Paul is saying: "Everywhere else 'head' means boss, chief executive officer, commander. But in the kingdom of God, the head is the person who comes under others, serving and building, and being willing to die for them."

In the church, Christ is more fully seen and experienced when we submit to Him as our head. And in grace-full relationships, a wife can come under her husband, and put to his service everything about herself that is *female* to enable her husband to become everything God created him to be. And a husband can come under his wife, bringing to bear everything about himself that is *male*, and in doing so he will enable his wife to become everything God created her to be. When we come under someone, we love and support—and we allow God to take the lead in changing and directing. We will see how this attitude has real and powerful application a little later.

If we obey the Scripture, "being subject to one another," we will have a relationship in which God can be seen—an image-of-God

---

[1] *The Subtle Power of Spiritual Abuse* (Minneapolis: Bethany House, 1991).

relationship. "For this cause [that God may be seen in our midst] a man shall leave his father and mother, and shall cleave to his wife; and the two shall become one flesh" (Ephesians 5:31). This is the description of the marriage relationship found in Genesis 2. Paul is using pre-fall, pre-curse language to describe the marriage relationship that results when our filling comes from the Spirit and not from ourselves. We are back to God's plan!

MEN, PAY ATTENTION

It is important to understand that this unconventional news lands more heavily on men than on anyone else. You have to hear this as an Ephesian male in order to hear what a significant confrontation this is between the kingdom of God and the kingdom of this world. For Paul to instruct wives to be under their husbands was new only in that now he was telling them how to do this from the heart as a result of being filled with the Spirit. They were already placed under their husbands as a function of their culture. But for a husband to come under his wife? To live as if the life of his wife was more precious than his very own? For him to nourish and cherish her as he would care for himself? This was unheard of.

Wives were there to keep the house and take care of the kids. Ephesian husbands went to other women for sex, companionship, even heightened religious experiences. This teaching went across the grain of everything an Ephesian man ever learned, every man-woman relationship he ever saw. He could *never* do this by trying hard; this heart transformation could only result as he struggled to depend on God to fill him.

For Paul to instruct children to be under their parents was also not new. Children were already under their parents as a function of a culture where people sold or killed children who did not live up to parental expectations. But for a father to place himself under his child? For him to stop short in his discipline when further discipline would provoke the child to anger—this was remarkable! The other fathers would think he was insane, less than a man, and not ruling over his household. To learn how to rule the spirit of your children, Paul is insisting, will take a work of the Holy Spirit. And it's important for us to see that Paul knew children could be filled with the Spirit in this way. This would result in a new ability to "arrange themselves under" their parents.

And for Paul to tell slaves to be under their masters was not new either. By law, slaves were already under their masters and required to obey and render service. This was a culture in which slaves were less than human, and were often killed for entertainment, much less disobedience. This was "new" to slaves only in that Paul was telling them to submit from the heart as a result of being filled with the Spirit. Fear was the old motivation. But what must the Ephesian men (only men could own property) have thought and felt when they read: "And, master, [submit to your slaves], and give up threatening, knowing that both their Master and yours is in heaven, and there is no partiality with Him" (Ephesians 6:9). For an Ephesian man to do this would take a filling of the Holy Spirit. At best, his peers would view him as a weakling, at worst—a lunatic.

A FINAL CONFRONTATION

Ultimately, what Paul has described here is a relationship of grace, freedom, and blessing—one that confronts the curse-full relationship described in Genesis 3. If you took a filled-with-the-Spirit, mutually submissive husband and wife and put them in Ephesus, their witness would confront every relationship in that city. And if you place this kind of marriage today in view of that part of the feminist movement that encourages women to have power by taking power, it will be a confrontation.

Then there are those in the body of Christ today who teach that God mediates His relationship with women *through* men. Look at a filled-with-the-Spirit, mutually submissive husband and wife next to that teaching and you will see quite a difference. And if you placed a mutually submissive, filled-with-the-Spirit husband and wife in a church of today, their presence would confront most marriages in that church.

By opening a different, more accurate understanding of Paul's teaching, I hope you have begun to acquire a new filter through which to view the marriage relationship. In later chapters we will see these principles in operation. Next, we will look at some of the ways relying on God continuously as our Source of fullness, as Paul instructs, will change the way you look at the job of parenting.

DISCUSSION QUESTIONS

1. *Describe what Paul means when he says to be filled with the Spirit.*

2. *Why do you think the verses about being filled with the Spirit (Ephesians 5:18–21) precede the verses about submission in marriage (Ephesians 5:22–23)?*

3. *After reading what the author has to say about it, explain what true submission in marriage is, both for the wife and for the husband.*

4. *How are other relationships changed by submission to one another (parent/child; servant/master)?*

8. Parenting Means Controlling Ourselves

Trying to control others is the first manifestation of the curse in relationships. And learning to control *ourselves* is the foundation stone in grace-full parenting.

PARENTING "BY THE BOOK"

This is the first of four chapters on what I call, "Parenting by the Book." I refer to it that way because the insights that I will present for dealing with children—that is, dealing with their spirits—flow right out of Scripture. There are two simple *Don't*s and two *Do*'s in this approach to parenting, and each will be covered in its own separate chapter. They are:

> *Don't* provoke your children to anger (Ephesians 6:4).
> *Do* bring them up in the discipline and instruction of the Lord (Ephesians 6:4).

Do train them up in the way they should go (Proverbs 22:6).
Don't cause the little ones to stumble (Luke 17:2).

FOCUSING ON YOUR OWN WORK

In counseling, as I have noted, I tend to see husbands who know more about the "wife" verses than the "husband" verses, and I've witnessed wives who know more about husband verses than wife verses. And they use their energy making sure the other person lives up to their verse.

Counselors see this phenomenon present in those relationships between parents and children in which the parents use Bible verses to shame and drive their children. Parents know all about the verses related to how children should behave but not so much about those that remind them about how they should behave. They remind their children, for instance, that Ephesians 6:1 says, "Children, obey your parents." But, parents, take a moment to notice something in Paul's words: He is addressing *children*, not parents. Likewise, he does not say, "Husbands, get your wives to submit to you," or "Wives, get your husbands to act like Christlike leaders." And he is not saying here, "Parents, get your kids to be obedient." This instruction is written *to* children, and misusing Scriptures written to others is like opening someone else's mail!

Parents, stay away from children's verses. We have our own verses to worry about. Our verse, Ephesians 6:4, says, "And, *fathers*, do not provoke your children to anger." We'll examine the rest of our verse, "Bring them up in the discipline and instruction of the Lord," in the next chapter.

UNDERSTANDING THE CONTEXT

"Do not provoke your children to anger"—this verse is addressed to fathers. Are fathers the only ones who ever provoke their children to anger? I don't think so. In the first-century Ephesian family, though, men were viewed as the ones with authority; hence the command was addressed to fathers. In a sense, the Ephesian families were not unlike many "chain-of-command" families of today, in that men hold the *position* of authority and get the final say, while women get to do all of the *work* of parenting. Regardless, the truth contained in this verse is this: Whoever is doing the parenting should not provoke their children to anger.

Is Paul telling parents they should never do or say anything about which their kids might feel angry? Not at all. Children are sometimes going to feel angry when they are asked to do things they'd rather *not* do. This may even be an often occurrence for some children. A person's anger is their own responsibility. Paul is not placing us in charge of controlling our children's anger, and some parents today mistakenly see it as their job to keep children happy all the time. Paul *is* placing us in charge of whether we provoke anger or not.

In fact, no parent is capable of controlling his/her child's anger. But we *are* capable of controlling whether we provoke them to anger.

WHAT IS ANGER?

To grasp the full impact of what Paul is saying, we must understand what anger is. There are several Greek words for "anger," three that we need to examine. The first word is *perigismos*, the word that appears in our Ephesians verse. It means "seething hostility," and it refers to anger that is forced to exist beneath the surface, or suppressed anger. Unfortunately, many Christians think this is what we are supposed to do with anger—just conceal it where it can't be seen. The text clearly shows that concealing anger is not a good thing to do.

The second word is *thumas*. This word is found in Galatians 5:20. It is translated "outbursts of anger," or anger that is explosive. This anger *results* from walking by the flesh. If you try to get your needs met, your life, value, and acceptance from people and material things instead of from the Spirit, you can count on frustration and resulting outbursts of anger. That is because people and material possessions hold out a false promise of fulfillment, but do not deliver.

The third word is *orgay*. It is the word found in Ephesians 4:26: "Be angry, and yet do not sin. . . ." (This word is also found in Ephesians 5:6, where it is translated *wrath*.) The first thing to note is that having this kind of anger is not automatically a sin. *Orgay* comes the closest to the pure experience of anger. This kind of anger is not good or bad. It is simply a signal that something important to us has been threatened or damaged. Our response to our anger is what is important, as we can see in the verse.

In other words, you can tell what is important to you by what you get angry about. If you become angry when someone scratches your car, it reveals the fact that your car is important to you. If you experience anger when someone slanders you, it simply means that your reputation is important to you. If you get angry when people treat others unjustly, it means that justice is important to you. If serving people in the kingdom of God is important to you, and you see leaders using their authority to serve themselves, you will become angry.

What does it mean, then, to be angry but not sin? It must be possible, or Paul's instruction makes no sense. Again, we must check the context. Paul says, "Therefore, laying aside falsehood, speak truth, each one of you, with his neighbor, for we are members of one another. Be angry, and yet do not sin; do not let the sun go down on your anger, and do not give the devil an opportunity" (Ephesians 4:25–26). I believe that Paul is telling us that when we are angry with someone, we are to go talk to that person.

Consequently, being angry at someone and *telling others instead* is to be angry and to sin. Being angry at someone and spreading rumors, giving negative hints in a conversation, or insulting them, is to be angry and to sin. In fact, the text demonstrates that being angry and doing nothing—letting "the sun go down on your anger"—is sinning. Ignored anger can grow into *perigismos* or *thumas*, neither of which is good. If you are angry with someone, talk to them.

There are Christians who believe that only some anger is justified—what they call "righteous indignation" or "holy anger." These are not scriptural terms. I think these phrases have been used by people who are "too spiritual" to have regular human anger, in order to shame others into concealing anger, as if this were more spiritual. This leads people into living a lie.

"DON'T PROVOKE . . . TO SEETHING HOSTILITY"

Our verse tells us that anger forced to remain under the surface is not good. If we are going to avoid provoking our children to seething anger, we need to recognize the ways we do so. Consider the following:

Not allowing our children to express their anger. The most obvious way to provoke children into a state of repressed anger is to not let them express it. If you ask your child to stop watching TV and perform a chore they were supposed to be doing, you may get an answer something like: "I'm really angry that I have to do this," or the child may simply show his anger by stomping or complaining. In response, many Christian parents would say, "Don't you ever let me hear you talk like that [or act like that]"; or "You are making Jesus sad by being angry"; or "Go to your room and don't come out until you can be polite." If so, you are provoking them to seething anger. They may decide to hide their anger in order to avoid the consequences of displeasing you—or because they think it's their job to make sure Jesus has a good day—or so that they can avoid having to go to their room. And when they respond to this kind of pressure, and do not show their anger, you may praise them and praise the Lord that you don't have an angry child—but don't get too excited. You simply have an angry kid with *perigismos*—that is, an expert at letting the sun go down on his anger.

Rather than provoke children to seething anger, it is better to acknowledge the fact that they are angry. Tell them that you appreciate their telling you about their anger, or the fact that they are angry, even though they may still be required to do the chore they don't like.

Often, rather than verbalize anger, a child will communicate it by behavior—for instance, they may storm away and slam the door. The problem is not the anger, but the manner in which it is expressed. The goal of discipline should be to help them express their anger "by the Book." If, for instance, your child storms off in anger and slams a door, say something like this: "I can see that you're angry with me. But it's not okay for you to run off and slam the door in my face. That doesn't help our relationship. If you're angry with me, say so. I can understand that you might be upset, but you still have to do your job."

Living with double standards. If it's not okay for the kids to litter, it's not okay for you. If you want them to care about the law, you have to keep the speed limit. (They can always tell when you don't.) If you want your children to care about God and church, but in your heart *you* don't—who are you kidding?

Here is an example of something that happened in my family. It happens to be about handling anger, but any double standard provokes seething. At five minutes to nine one night, we were on our way home from a friend's lake home. We were six tired, sunburned shadows of our former selves, squeezed into a Dodge Colt hatchback. I looked ahead to my left and noticed that we were coming up to a store that sold sofas and recliner-rockers. We had been looking for a sofa for some time. I put on my left turn signal and announced, "Look, that store is still open. Let's go in and look at sofas." Ignoring the children's pleas for mercy, I turned into the parking lot.

Holly and I went into the store, followed—much to my chagrin— by a line of four frustrated, lobster-colored daughters. They should have been home in bed moaning about their sunburns, instead of here in this store moaning about their sunburns. As we talked to the salesperson, all the girls disappeared into the far reaches of the showroom.

The store was huge like a warehouse. Just as we were discussing some facts with the clerk, I noticed some distant movement, and looked to a far corner of the store where I saw our daughters. It looked like a tidal wave had struck fifty square feet of otherwise tranquil recliner-rockers. The salesperson shot me one of those looks.

The anger rose up from my toes, stopping with a taste of bile at the back of my mouth. First I faked the fruit of the Spirit for the salesperson (after all, I am a Christian, and a licensed counselor at that). I dragged up the best love, joy, peace, and patience I could muster—then excused myself and went to tame the wave of lurching chairs.

When they saw me coming, all four girls ceased every sign of life and tried to become part of the chairs. With teeth clenched I hissed, "That's it! You're going to the car. What's wrong with you?!" I grabbed the first arm I could find and led my little shame-squad to their prison on wheels. Then I went back to Holly and the salesperson, faked some more fruit of the Spirit, and finished our conversation.

On the way home, the inside of the Dodge Colt was deathly quiet. All four girls had broken a sweat. Then one of them broke the silence. "Dad," she whispered, "can I ask you a question?"

A question? I ask the questions around here. . . . I was starting to scare myself with my thoughts. *Calm down.*

"Yes," I replied bitingly. "You can ask me a question."

"Well, Dad," she said timidly, "how come when we are angry with you, you want us to say it with words? But when you're angry with us, you can just grab us and make us sit in the car?"

Yeah, Jeff, how come? You can imagine I was seething—not at this child so much as at the voice of Truth that was asking me the same question. *How come?* I thought. *Because I'm the dad.* Bad answer. *Because I'm an adult.* Bad answer. *Because I'm bigger, faster, stronger, louder . . .* Bad answer. *Because I don't have to do what I say.* Bad answer. Frankly, there was no good enough reason.

I drove in speechless conviction for the rest of the ride. When we got home, we all sat down in the living room together. I felt guilty for having lived a double standard before them. Yes, the girls had made a poor choice—but I had controlled their behavior, not mine, and I felt sad. I hadn't given them a chance to respond to the confrontation; I hadn't explained that I was angry with them and why. I was wrong, and I apologized. Letting the sun go down with this kind of question, leaving it unanswered, provokes children to seething hostility—and later, at some time, to open rebellion.

Speaking, thinking, and feeling for your kids. When they were little, three out of four of our daughters had feet that were flat as pancakes. We're talking about very expensive shoes here. Their shoes had to have a special feature called a *Thomas Heel* so that their legs didn't tip in.

One summer day, when Erin was four years old, I took her to one of the few shoe stores in Minneapolis that carried the kind of shoes we needed. We were on a quest for sandals that had the right kind of heel. The store had several pairs in her size, and after about half an hour she had tried them all on.

As we were talking about which sandals she liked out of those that fit, a young mother with her own four-year-old came into the store. The two of them sat next to us and the mother said to the clerk, "Do you have any Thomas Heel sandals that would fit a four-year-old?" I could hardly believe it. The clerk measured the little girl's feet, and then pointed to the pile of sandals lying on the floor in front of us. The mother was a little flabbergasted.

Erin was still hemming and hawing, and we watched as the little girl next to us tried on a beautiful, braided leather pair, decorated with colored beads. They didn't fit. Then she tried on a second pair—not very pretty, but not bad as Thomas Heel shoes go. They didn't fit either. Then she tried on a plain, ugly pair that fit like Cinderella's glass slippers. The mom immediately said, "We'll take these."

The little girl then pitched a fit. She screamed, whined, pleaded, and finally threw herself on the floor. All the time the girl was doing this the mother was holding up the ugly pair and saying to her daughter, "Oh, we like these sandals, don't we? And don't we think they're beautiful?"

Erin was looking at the woman with a peculiar, scrunched-up expression on her face that seemed to be saying, *Look, lady, we four-year-olds know ugly sandals when we see them. Who are you kidding?* I have to admit that I was a little confused about who the "we" was that this lady was talking about. She must have had a mouse in her pocket who concurred with her assessment of the sandals, because her daughter certainly didn't agree.

That little girl was sad and angry because she couldn't get the sandals she wanted. And the more the mother tried to fix her disappointment, the angrier the child got. And the more her mom tried to get her to conceal her anger, the more furious she grew.

True, we parents would like it if our kids would just accept our answers without a fuss. And we wish they wouldn't make scenes in public. We get embarrassed and start worrying about what other people are thinking. Sometimes, in fact, I think kids act certain ways at times *just* to see the look of horror on our face.

But I don't believe there is much point in analyzing the little girl's anger at not getting the sandals she wanted. Granted, people get angry sometimes when they don't get what they want. And we are right to be concerned if our children respond with anger too often. A child's initial anger at a parent's decision is not that catastrophic; if a parent has reasons for making a choice, she should stick to her guns and explain her reasons to the child in a simple manner.

But when a mom or dad *repeatedly discount* a child's feelings, then there is cause for real alarm. The mounting anger of this little girl was provoked by a mom who acted as if she knew how her daughter *really* felt and what she *really* wanted better than the daughter did. In addition, there was a place in this scenario where the mother and daughter agreed. They were both disappointed at not being able to get the pretty sandals. How much better it would have been for the mother to say, "I know you're disappointed to not get the pretty sandals. So am I. But when it comes to shoes, fit is what counts. So we're going to get these others instead."

Violating children's boundaries. Though some adults disagree, children need to have privacy. My oldest daughter used to have a sign on her door that proclaimed, "Enter, and die!" To Holly and me, this was not a big deal. She was not saying, "You are not worthy to enter my room, so stay away." She was not trying to be sneaky. She was simply declaring, "This is my personal space, and if you get to come in it's because I decide I will let you."

One of my jobs as a parent is to respect my daughters' boundaries and, in fact, to help them build strong ones. If I open the door without permission—because "I pay the bills" or because "It's my house"—I am disrespecting my daughter.

It is okay for kids to decide not to share. *Sharing* means that a child *owns* something, and that lending it will bring someone else joy, or will be helpful to them. Some parents make their children share for the wrong reasons. It may be that they are tired of the other child's whining. Or because it will look selfish not to share. If a child parts with his/her possession only to avoid punishment, he/she is complying merely to avoid pain. A child's yes really is not a yes, unless a no is really an option for that child. And trying to force a child's yes provokes seething anger.

Turning a deaf ear. "Every child should have the chance to defend his or her innocence before being disciplined. Circumstances of which we're unaware might make a difference in our response to this misbehavior," says Paul Lewis.[1]

We need to *listen* to our children. We need to give them a say in things that affect them. Why? Because it communicates trust and the message that we think they are capable of some thought and choice. Sometimes they know what is right; sometimes we are

---

[1] *40 Ways to Teach Your Child Values* (Downers Grove, IL: Tyndale, 1985).

wrong. Sometimes it is not that they want their way; they just want to be heard and respected. The little girl with the sandals was not listened to in the least. And children seethe when adults show them no respect.

When parents are "absent." About ten years ago I was engulfed in the idolatry of ministry, as described in chapter 5. One day as I prepared to leave town for another seminar, I realized that I didn't want to go. As I sat on the living room floor repacking my suitcase with clean clothes, I began to cry. I had said yes to too much traveling, and now I missed my family and wanted with all my heart to stay home.

Erin, who was very little at the time, saw me crying. She walked over to me, put her arm around my neck, and laid her head on my shoulder. In an attempt to comfort me she said, "Don't worry, Daddy. We won't ever forget you."

This was only slightly comforting. Mostly, it was a confrontation that brought about a turning point in my struggle to blend family life and ministry.

I realized that she was right. They wouldn't forget me—but what they would *remember* was a dad who thought ministry was more important than they were. The psalmist says, "Behold, children are a gift of the Lord; the fruit of the womb is a reward" (127:3). They are important enough to be around for. When you neglect to spend time with your children, they feel hurt, angry, and like they don't matter. Some parents only know what's happening in their children's lives because they hear about it, not because they were there to see it.

If you are the kind of parent who is not around enough to hear about your children's needs—or if you force them into silence when they do speak up about your absence—you are causing them to seethe with anger.

When we "shame" our children. Tired of Trying to Measure Up is the book I wrote to help people recover from the effects of shame. When people receive messages about themselves that they are *defective, unloved, worthless,* and that they can *never measure up,* their basic identity is formed around a horribly wounded self-image. The actions of the mom in the sandal story sent messages to her daughter that she was helpless, useless, and small. Under these circumstances, anyone who is normal will experience *orgay* anger.

Suppose that mother took the little girl out of the store and spanked her for her display? Rather than addressing basic issues with our children, we often use the whole weight of our authority to point out how defective they are: "You made a fuss—and the problem is *you*. What a rebellious, miserable, embarrassing child you are. You're so awful I'm ashamed to be seen in public with you." This crushes a child's spirit, and leaves them seething with unresolved conflict and anger.

By now I hope you can see how real and how deep is the problem of provoking our children to anger. Yes, even with a new approach to parenting they may still respond in anger. *But getting anger into hiding is not what Christian parenting is about.*

In chapter 9, we will see how Christian parents can create an atmosphere where children can learn to depend upon God for growth and change—for this *is* our task, in the Lord.

DISCUSSION QUESTIONS

1. *Define anger. What does Scripture mean when it says: "Be angry and sin not"?*

2. *What are some ways we can provoke our children to anger?*

3. *List some alternate ways to deal with a child's "acting out" his anger.*

4. *Describe a better way to deal with the child's anger when she couldn't get the sandals she wanted.*

9. Building Faith Into Your Children

About eight years ago, Holly took a trip to visit some old friends from her growing-up days. She carried with her a certain amount of anxiety, because she had some difficult things she felt she needed to say. She knew they saw things very differently and that there would be tension. In particular, it had always been difficult to be around these folks because they sent out definite signals that she was a second-rate commodity. Holly tried to stay hopeful about the visit, but mostly she was worried and afraid. "You'll be okay," I said as I watched her leave—and I hoped I was right.

Later that night, after the kids were in bed, the telephone rang. It was Holly, and she sounded great. "You sound like you're doing fine. Things must be okay."

"I am," she replied. "I just opened my suitcase and found a letter that Kara hid in my clothes." Kara is our oldest daughter who was about ten years old at the time. "Her note really gave me a boost."

This is what Kara wrote:

Dear Mom,
    I love you. I know this is a hard trip for you. I think it's neat that you care about your friends enough to try to talk to them. I know that they might make fun of you. Just remember, Jesus is who makes you special.

Yours truly,
Your daughter Kara

In 1 Timothy 6:12, Paul says, "Fight the good fight of faith." Our little girl was echoing the apostle Paul. She was giving her mom what we had been giving her for ten years—a reminder to draw her inner life and worth from Jesus.

MORE ABOUT "OUR VERSE"

The second aspect of true, spiritual parenting is also found in Ephesians 6:4, in what I call "the parent verse": "Bring [your children] up in the discipline and instruction of the Lord."

I used to think Paul was saying, "Get your children to be good rule-followers. Teach them how to act." Following rules *is* important, as is learning how to live. But I don't believe, in light of Paul's teaching about spiritual filling, this verse is about rule-keeping. I believe Paul is saying: "Bring your children along in the fight of faith. Help them learn to really hang on to Jesus." This is where we step in to help our children learn how to allow themselves to keep being filled with the Spirit.

Most Christian parents focus on the words *discipline* and *instruction*, and overlook the *bring up* part. "Bring up" has uplifting, nurturing, serving connotations. We are not to beat down or force into. It is not our job to turn our children into Christian replicas of Pavlov's dogs, barking out the right Bible verse for every occasion. Rather, we are to build them into deeply faithful adults.

OUR CHILDREN'S BIGGEST FIGHT

As a pastor and counselor, I know that our children's biggest struggle is exactly the same as ours: We are all fighting to draw our sense of significance, have our real needs met, and view ourselves as loved and accepted on the basis of Christ's performance and not our own. Unfortunately—as it is with many Christian adults—that fight has been lost for our children in the preoccupation with performance that is so prevalent in Christian families and churches.

I want to emphasize: It is not that behaviors don't matter. Learning to make right choices matters a great deal. Obedience to the things of God is not optional, it is mandatory. But it is also simply consistent with the fullness we have in Christ. Let me illustrate.

Paul says, in Ephesians 3:17–19:

> May your roots go down deep into the soil of God's marvelous love; and may you be able to feel and understand, as all God's children should, how long, how wide, how deep, and how high his love really is; and to experience this love for yourselves, though it is so great that you will never see the end of it or fully know or understand it. And so at last you will be filled up with God himself. (TLB)

This passage is all about being full on the inside. God is the Source of our filling.

In John 4, we find the story of a Samaritan woman Jesus met one day at a well. Jesus offered this woman living water. This was a person who was trying to fill her inner emptiness in relationships with men. Jesus said to her, "Whoever drinks of the water that I shall give him shall never thirst; but the water that I shall give him shall become in him a well of water springing up to eternal life" (v. 14). And later, speaking to a whole crowd, Jesus reiterates: "If any man is thirsty, let him come to Me and drink. He who believes in Me, as the Scripture said, 'From his innermost being shall flow rivers of living water'" (John 7:37–38).

Jesus has promised to put a well on the inside of us, and from that inner well life will flow. Our simple task is to remember to drink from that well instead of from all the wells that promise to fill us but never can. Being good athletically, having lots of friends, being in a relationship with a member of the opposite sex, achieving good grades, or being captain of the church quiz team cannot fill our children. We need the well on the inside, and so do our children. We need to allow ourselves to be filled daily, minute by minute, with the Spirit, and so do our children.

Wouldn't you like to help your children learn how to recognize their thirst for Jesus Christ? Wouldn't you like to help them find that Jesus is the only one who can give them life, from the inside?

THE DISCIPLINE OF FAITH

It is interesting to compare the books of Galatians and Colossians. Paul was angry at the Galatians. His letter to them is a scathing confrontation of the fact that they had been "walking by the flesh" instead of the Spirit. But the "flesh" for the Galatians was not pornography, drunkenness, or thievery. The Galatians had begun to measure their acceptance spiritually by whether or not they performed certain religious behaviors. They let religious performance direct the way they acted, instead of allowing the Spirit to do so. Paul calls this "walking in the flesh."

To the Colossians, on the other hand, Paul says this:

> For even though I am absent in body, nevertheless I am with you in spirit, rejoicing to see your good discipline and the stability of your faith in Christ. As you therefore have received Christ Jesus the Lord, so walk in Him, having been firmly rooted and now being built up in Him and established in your faith. (Colossians 2:5–7)

Paul was excited to see their stability and discipline. But he wasn't complimenting them on their perfect church attendance, tithing, or daily devotions. Yes, these are all good practices, but Paul was rejoicing in their spiritual stability, which was rooted in their faith in Jesus. Unlike the Galatians, they were hanging on to Jesus.

Paul urged the Colossians to keep living in Christ the same way they came to Him in the first place—by faith. Jesus was the soil their "faith roots" were planted in, and this living faith is what would continue to build them up.

FAITH-BUILDING OPPORTUNITIES

Callie came home on the bus one day and said that a bunch of kids were making fun of her. She was sad and scared, and wanted to find a different ride to school. In our talk with her, we acknowledged her feelings and supported her in her sadness. We also wanted to find a way to remind her to hang on to Jesus.

"Those kids sure are acting like you're not very special. When they treat you that way how do you feel?" we asked.

This brought tears, and we hugged her to offer comfort.

"So, on this hand, are the kids who say you are little and dumb," I said. "And on this hand, is Jesus. He says you're special and capable, and if He was picking a team He'd pick you first. So now you have to decide who you're going to believe."

Callie has had to decide many times whose voice she was going to listen to for her sense of worth. There is no doubt that sometimes, like you and me, she has chosen to listen to the wrong voice. That is our fight of faith, ongoing—to resist the temptation to find our life in anything and anyone but Christ. But Callie is growing, just as we are.

Let's face facts: Even if our children begin their own faith journey and choose to believe they are loved and accepted by God because of Jesus' work on the cross, it does not mean other kids are going to be transformed into nice people. And it doesn't mean our children won't feel hurt when hurtful things are said or done to them. But we can stop trying to control behaviors and feelings, and focus on value and identity. *Our eternal value and identity are settled because of Christ.*

But let's say that Callie decided her value really was determined by older, stronger kids. She might come up with a plan, "If I can just do this or not do that, then they'll finally like me." Our job, as parents, might not be to talk her out of the plan. Our job may be to teach her by using the plan.

We could say, "Okay, you try to get special by pleasing these kids for two weeks. Do everything you think they want you to do. And don't do anything they wouldn't like. At the end of the two weeks, we'll talk." My guess is that at the end of the two weeks, a tired Callie would have pleased a lot of people—but she would not feel any more special on the inside.

Let me say it plainly: Our job as Christian parents is simply to draw our children's attention to what is real—what is true—and not to try to control how they feel.

Training your children about this thirst for life and significance has many practical values, as an unusual incident with our daughter Jesi showed us.

One day, Jesi came home from school and told us she'd been challenged to a fight by another girl on the bus.

"Decline the invitation," we suggested.

But the next day, after school, Holly looked out the front window and saw dozens of kids on our lawn.

"What's this all about?" Holly asked Jesi, who was just coming downstairs.

"She challenged me again today," Jesi replied.

"What did you tell her?" asked Holly.

"I said, 'Yeah, right,'" Jesi told her. Evidently the girl had taken that for a "yes."

Now a crowd had showed up for the fight! They had signs and pom-poms, and one kid even had a bugle. (No kidding.)

Holly charged out the front door and loudly announced that

the fight had been canceled. After seeing that Holly was even more blood-thirsty than they were—"They're *not* going to get my baby!"— the disappointed crowd of kids dispersed.

That evening, we talked with Jesi about what was happening. "You must really be a powerful person, Jes," we suggested.

"What do you mean?"

"Well, that other girl is spending so much energy and time on you. So it must be really important to her what you think."

"Hmmm," purred Jes, considering.

The next day, the same girl started in on Jesi again. "I must really be a powerful person," Jesi suggested.

"What do you mean?" the other girl asked.

"Well, you're spending so much time and energy on me it must be really important to you what I think."

"Hmmm," growled the girl, considering.

She never bothered Jesi again. Even this child, who knew nothing about the filling of the Spirit, knew that she would not really feel any more important if she beat up Jesi VanVonderen.

Here is another practical example:

When our Kara was in fourth grade, she tested into a program at her school that allowed her to participate in some alternative learning experiences. Two years later, Erin entered fourth grade. She really wanted to be able to be in the same program, and so she took the same tests. Because of her scores on the test, she was not allowed into the program. Erin was devastated. She felt sad and defective.

"What's wrong with me?" she cried. "I really wanted to be in that program." She felt so sad that she took the initiative to go and talk to the school social worker about how she was feeling.

That night when she came home from school I asked her how she was feeling. "A little better. I talked to the school counselor today and she told me about IALAC," she replied.

"IALAC? What's that?" I asked.

"Well, the counselor wrote IALAC on a piece of paper and

handed it to me. She told me it stood for 'I Am Lovable and Capable.' Then she took it back and crumpled it up. She said that sometimes things happen and we don't feel very lovable and capable. Then she smoothed it out and handed it back. She said that when that happens, we just need to smooth it out the best we can and go on."

"That's kind of a cool example," I said. "But, in fact, we have something even better than that. Jesus' love for us isn't like a piece of paper. It's more like steel."

"I told the same story to Mom," Erin interjected. "And she said Jesus' love is like the hardest gem, like a diamond."

The next day, I went to a store that sells plaques. I had them engrave a metal plaque for Erin (I couldn't afford diamonds), and put a piece of plexiglas over the engraving so it wouldn't get scratched. The plaque said:

YALAC
You are in my program.
Love, J.C.

When I gave the plaque to Erin, I told her that the plexiglas might get scratched because sometimes things happen. But the message of love underneath will never change, never be damaged, and never disappear. It's great to be recognized and get in special programs. But Jesus is the one who makes us important.

Each day presents every parent with many opportunities to help their children fight the fight of faith. Our children are not short of opportunities to chase empty promises in the vain attempt to meet their inner needs—whether it is the offer of drugs, or sex, or the chance to belong to the most popular peer group.

Remember, empty things don't need to be evil to be empty. Getting good grades isn't evil. But grades don't have the power to establish a person's worth. Neither does earning the approval of your parents, or perfect attendance pins for going to Sunday school. In addition, the media, peers, even sometimes family and the church bombard children with shaming messages that say something is wrong with them. We need to watch for ways to encourage our children to look to Jesus alone as their source of value and acceptance.

THE IMPORTANCE OF MODELING

I think Scripture displays an even more powerful way of conveying the way we draw life from Jesus Christ: It is absolutely essential for us as parents to fight the faith fight ourselves, so that our children see us struggling with the same issues and winning. I am talking about being living models of faith.

Deuteronomy shows us the pattern for bringing up our children "in the discipline and instruction of the Lord." Look at it:

> Hear, O Israel! The Lord is our God, the Lord is one! And you shall love the Lord your God with all your heart and with all your soul and with all your might. (Deuteronomy 6:4–5)

This is the message we must pass on: *Have one God.* Don't try to get your inner needs met from a bunch of puny, substitute, false gods. Love and be loved by our one, true God, with every ounce of strength. In fact, that is what it will take!

> And these words, which I am commanding you today, shall be on your heart. (Deuteronomy 6:6)

This is the method, *step number one,* for communicating the message: *Write it on your heart.* The message that God is our life must be the message written on the tablets of our heart before it can be our children's message.

> And you shall teach them diligently to your sons and shall talk of them when you sit in your house and when you walk by the way and when you lie down and when you rise up. And you shall bind them as a sign on your hand and they shall be as

frontals on your forehead. And you shall write them on the doorposts of your house and on your gates. (Deuteronomy 6:7–9)

Step number two: Pass on to your children the message that has first been ingrained in your heart. Pass on timeless truth that it is a fight to have one God. Let your faith in one God flow out from inside you; let it be displayed in everything you do outwardly as a result.

MODELING IN THE NEW TESTAMENT

It's obvious that the apostle Paul believed in the importance of modeling. In Philippians he says, "The things which you have learned and received and heard and seen in me, practice these things" (4:9). In 2 Thessalonians, Paul offers himself as a model, so that we might follow his example. He not only modeled, he drew attention to himself as a model.

First Corinthians 11 portrays an incredible picture of Paul as a model of the faith. Here he says, "Be imitators of me, just as I also am of Christ" (v. 1).

My wife has taught me about the richness of this verse. She is an actress in the art of mime. In the translation, the word *imitator* comes from the Greek word *mimetai*.

Holly told me one day that the art of mime comes from the concept of *mimetai*. I said, "You mean like when we do charades?"

"No, not at all," she replied. "Charades is pantomime. Pantomime means indicating something on the outside, so that someone else can see and experience it. It's like pretending there is a wall, so others can see the wall. To do mime, I have to see and experience the wall myself. What appears on the outside is not for the benefit of those looking on. It is an expression of what I experience inwardly."

Consider this, and I believe it will give new depth to what Paul is saying to the Corinthians. He is not telling Christians to copy his external Christian behavior. Looking Christian on the outside *so that others will see* also misses the point. Paul is, rather, instructing us to focus on an internal reality, out of which will flow its expression.

WHAT MODELING LOOKS LIKE

To further illustrate, I want to close this chapter by giving you examples of what it looks like to model the fight of faith. You can let your children in on your struggle. The side benefit is that they will get to know you better. Here are just a few examples of what it means to model this inner struggle to hold on to Jesus.

At work. In 1980, I quit my job at a treatment center that began caring more about politics and money than people. I did not have another job waiting in the wings. We had only a small financial reserve to live on. Our girls wondered if we were going to wind up as street people. Here is the essence of what Holly and I told them: "Dad has decided to quit his job. He doesn't agree with the way people are being treated there. This is really scary because we don't have a lot of money. In fact, Dad stayed longer than he should have stayed, because his job made him feel safe. But we don't trust jobs or money for our needs. We trust Jesus. He will keep us safe. So we're choosing to hang on to Him instead of Dad's job right now." And do you know what? God was faithful. We were safe. And my kids got to see that too.

In the ministry. Occasionally I have an extremely hard confrontation to make in a counseling session. I feel afraid, maybe even a little nauseous. My family notices that something is up. One of my daughters will say, "Hey, Dad, why are you acting so strange?"

I try to give an answer that models faith: "Because I have a hard thing to do. And I'm worried that some people won't like me. They might think I'm stupid and not good at what I do. But they don't decide the truth about me—Jesus decides. So I'm going through with it, even though I'm scared. I'd like you to pray that I remember that when I get in the counseling room."

In parenting. Sometimes I overreact to something one of my daughters does in public because I feel embarrassed and I'm worried about what people think of me as a dad. Here's a faith-modeling apology: "I apologize for losing my temper with you. I was concerned about how you were acting. But what I was more concerned about is what people were thinking about me. And I took it out on you. I'm sorry."

With the schools. When one of our daughters was in second grade, she was having a very difficult time reading. One day she came home from school looking very sad. We asked her what was wrong and, choking back tears, she told us what happened.

"After I finished reading out loud today, the teacher said, 'What's wrong with you? Did you forget to learn how to read in first grade?' "

After giving her a hug, here was our faith-modeling response: "We can tell you're really sad. Do you know what? You are really capable, and we know you'll catch on to reading. We've decided to have a talk with your teacher. This is what we are going to tell him: 'We're happy that you're concerned with our daughter's reading. We are too. But it's not okay for you to make her feel terrible because of the way she reads.' "

Our little girl caught up in reading. At the end of that year of school, the teacher approached Holly and me to tell us that our daughter had done fine in reading. He also thanked us, and told us he'd learned to be more careful with the words he used.

In relating to your family of origin. Let's say one or both of your parents is upset by the way your children are acting at their house. They say shaming things to them and insinuate that something must be wrong with them—and with you, as a parent, for that matter. Your faith-modeling confrontation might go like this: "This is your house, and it's fine for you to object to how the kids are acting. And you can ask them to change their behavior. But it's not okay to belittle them—or me—because they don't act the way you'd prefer. I love my kids, and I'd like you to treat them with respect. If you'd like, we could work together on coming up with some wise consequences for teaching them about their behavior."

It's too bad when you have to protect your kids from being torn down by their own relatives—but being a relative does not give someone license to say hurtful things.

Pass on to your children the treasure of knowing how to hold on to Jesus Christ—to the life and value that come from believing in His love for us. This *is* our children's most important fight. And we as Christian parents are their most significant allies.

"Bring them up in the discipline and instruction of the Lord." *Do it.* And remember it begins as you fight your own fight of faith; you can't give away something you don't have, and being a living sermon is better than being just a long-winded one.

Now we'll take a look, in chapter 10, at the concept of setting children free to be who God created them to be. You'll be delighted to see them become the people you've always wanted them to be too!

DISCUSSION QUESTIONS

1. *Why is it important to teach children that their value and identity are settled because of Christ's work on the cross?*

2. *Teaching children how to live is more than a set of rules to obey. How important is living example to a child? Give some ways to "show" a child how to live.*

3. *Give examples of modeling the fight of faith—first from the book, and then from your own experience.*

4. *How important is it to stand up for our children when they are wrongly accused or spoken to in a demeaning way? Give examples.*

10. Freeing Your Children's Hearts

Everything I ever needed to know about parenting I learned in canine obedience school—well, not quite. But now that I've gotten your attention, I did learn a couple of things as a result of training my dog to fetch. Let me tell you what I mean.

I have a black Labrador retriever named Mitzi. Holly and the girls bought her for me as a surprise Father's Day present. They almost got me the Chesapeake Bay retriever with "a good nose." This is the kind of dog that examines every visitor who comes in the door—the kind that digs up every stick, bone, acorn, tin can, and angleworm it detects anywhere under the first two feet of topsoil. Normandy Beach after D-Day pales in comparison to the lawns of men who own dogs with "good noses." Mitzi has worked out well. She is too ladylike for such antics.

I decided that I wanted to train her to retrieve, so I acquired a training video. While the instructor shared many helpful training insights, one thing he said made the greatest impression: "You don't have to teach a retriever to retrieve. Retrievers already know how to retrieve, hence the name *retriever.*" I stopped the tape and thought about that. He was right. Mitzi was a retrieving fool. She already retrieved everything you threw for her, and quite a few things you didn't. "You have to create an environment in which your retriever can learn to be the retriever it already is," the instructor concluded.

Parenting is *not* like training a dog, though some psychologists would have us believe this is so. Training animals is mostly about behavior modification, teaching them how to respond in relation to punishments and rewards. Parenting is about discipline—that is *discipling,* or teaching children to make understanding choices out of wisdom.

Yes, I do agree that it is necessary to create a learning environment, and this is the third aspect of "parenting by the Book." As Christian parents, we can best help our children by honoring their individuality and by building on the ways God has made them different from one another.

How can we create a family environment where children can become all that God created them to be?

DISCOVERING THEIR "WAY"

In northern Minnesota there is an area called the Boundary Waters Canoe Area. It is a place that has been set aside by law to be preserved as a wilderness. Motorized travel, building, and logging are limited. It is a natural setting in which you can view a variety of animals—moose, timber wolves, loons, beavers, and eagles. One day, several years ago, I was floating around in a canoe in this area, and I spotted an eagle. I was utterly amazed as I watched it climb, soar, dive for fish, and then climb again. It made me think sadly of eagles I had seen in captivity. I couldn't help thinking, *What an incredible bird an eagle is when it's allowed to be an eagle.* Eagles have a "way" about them.

Proverbs 22:6 says, "Train up a child in the *way* he should go, and even when he is old he will not depart from it." "In the way" is translated from words that more literally say, *according to his way.* Children have a way about them too, just like eagles.

CREATING AN ENVIRONMENT IN WHICH TO *BECOME*

The word that is translated "train up," in the verse from Proverbs, is a word also used to describe the way a midwife interacted with a newborn baby in those days. She would dip her finger in sweet grape or fig juice and massage the palate of the infant. This would stimulate the urge to suck. Though natural in newborns, sometimes they need a jump-start. If you have had a newborn, or cared for one, you know that for a while sucking is what they like to do most! But sometimes you have to gently stroke the side of their face to get them interested.

Getting a baby interested in something they already love to do: Now you have the flavor of "training up" a child in his own way. This is not about creating an environment conducive to the behavioral results *you* want. It is not about programming behaviors.

How, then, do we train up our children in their own way? This is accomplished by creating an environment in which they can

- learn to respect their own sexuality and that of others.
- learn to become competent at their developmental jobs.
- learn to live consistently with their unique identity as people.
- learn to live consistently with their identity in Christ.

TRAINING THEM TO RESPECT SEXUALITY

Girls and boys are equally special. Many families have unspoken rules that say boy-children are more special than girl-children, or vice versa. One woman told me that when she was a teenager, every time she asked her parents if she could drive the car, she was told that she would have to check with her brother first because he might want to use it. The problem was that it was not the brother's car; it was the parents' car! The message given: *Boys are more special (or more important) than girls.* Of course, this is not true.

In another family, every time the little boy-cousins are around, the aunt and uncle lament in front of their daughters that they wished they'd had a boy. It's fine to wish you had a girl or a boy. Just be careful of the message you send to the children you *do* have.

The following statements communicate disrespect on the basis of sexuality:

> You're pretty good at science—for a girl.
> For a guy, you have pretty good taste in clothes.

The rule is, *think* about the messages you send to your children.

And be very careful of the *generalizations* you make about the sexes: All men are not irresponsible, untrustworthy jerks just because they are male (like your insensitive father, or uncle). All men aren't interested in just one thing (just because you were sexually abused). All women aren't oversensitive (just because you had a mother who controlled the family with her emotional outbursts). Think about the messages you are sending your kids, based on your own biased attitudes.

Girls and boys are equally special—and they are equally accountable, equally capable, and equally sensitive. Girls don't get off the hook because they are cute. They are responsible for their choices. "Boys will be boys" is sometimes used as an excuse for behavior that is inappropriate for anyone, male or female.

The late Harry Chapin wrote a song called "Why Do the Little Girls?" In it he asked the question: "Why do the little girls grow crooked, while the little boys grow tall?" He suggests many answers, including this: "The boys were taught to reach for the stars, the girls to reach the shelves." This should *never* be true in grace-full families.

If I had sons, I would offer to take them hunting, fishing, and camping. If they didn't like those things, we would find things to do together that we all liked. I have daughters, and I offer to take them hunting, fishing, and camping. If they don't like those things, we find other things to do together that we all like. But I offer. They get to say no if they don't want to go. I ask, even though they are girls. *Not* asking because they are girls would send them a message that girls are not as special as boys (or as versatile), or that they are not as welcomed in my world. And girls *are* as special.

When my daughters are sad about something, I give them a hug. I tell them that it's okay to cry when they're sad. I let them know I'm *with* them. If I had sons I would do the same. Men who are not sensitive are often that way because they were told loud and clear as boys that there is something wrong with boys who feel sad. If I had sons, they would be allowed to have their anger and express it. When my daughters are angry, I encourage them to tell me about it. I remind them that they are capable of making wise choices, even when they are angry. Women who are depressed are often that way because they were told as girls that there is something wrong with girls who express strong emotions—like anger.

RESPECTING DIFFERENCES

Then there are ways that daughters and sons are *different*.

A few years ago our nephew Casey flew here to the Midwest for two weeks during the summer to stay with us at a cottage on a lake. That visit turned out to be quite an educational experience for our family. It's true that I was a teenage boy once, but I don't remember anything vaguely compared to what I saw when Casey was here.

When our four daughters awakened in the morning, they lounged in bed and listened to the birds for a while. Then they crawled out of bed and moved with their blankets to the living room, where they got into more lounging. Eventually, they got hungry and moseyed to the kitchen to forage for something to eat. Each of them concocted their own version of breakfast. One morning one had cereal, another eggs, another toast and peanut butter, and the last a bagel. With breakfast in hand, they'd mosey back to the living room for some further lounging. No hurry here. After all, it was summer vacation.

Not so with Casey. Casey didn't wake up and listen to the birds. He was up *before* the birds. Then, like a Stealth Bomber on a secret mission, he glided undetected into the kitchen where he descended on any box of sugar-sweetened cereal he could find. With the efficiency of a highly skilled cat burglar, Casey was *in* and *out*. No mess, no evidence. Just an empty space where the cereal used to be.

And Casey did not sit down to eat. The guy did not sit down. He simply bent over the countertop and placed his elbows on each side of the cereal bowl. Without lifting his head or elbows, he poured the cereal and milk into the bowl, grabbed the spoon and started to eat. One *double-the-normal-human-speed* bite followed another, until all of the cereal in the bowl—and in the box—was gone.

The point is, the difference between Casey and my daughters is one of *style*, not a matter of which is the better way to *be*.

TRAINING THEM TO BE COMPETENT FOR THEIR AGE

A few years ago we moved into a house that a contractor had built for himself. He'd built a sauna in the basement for those Minnesota winter evenings when he came home from a day outdoors and needed to thaw out. Neither Holly nor I particularly like saunas. I can't breathe in them. But because we owned one we felt obliged to take advantage of it.

One day while we were in there sweltering—I mean enjoying ourselves—Callie appeared in the doorway. She was three at the time, and clad only in her underwear. She announced that she'd come to join us. After about twenty seconds of sitting there with us, she stood up and declared, "This can't be good for children *or* adults." And she left. Holly and I looked at each other—and then we left too. Not long after, we tore out the sauna and incorporated the space into a bedroom.

This illustration is not about saunas, it's about the fact that Callie, at three, was doing her job: In general, it is the job of children to notice things and learn about the world. *What is real? What is normal? What hurts? What feels good?* Children are great observers. And they can draw very good conclusions from what they observe, *if* they are allowed to do their jobs.

A friend of mine told me a sad thing about the way his mother related to his children. "My mom liked my kids until they turned two," he confided. "As soon as they learned to say no, it was like she didn't want anything to do with them. Whenever they would say no, or even ask why, she would say, 'My, doesn't that child have a mind of his own!'

"Now that my son is thirteen and wants to wear shoes like his friends, she says, 'What's wrong with him? Doesn't that child have a mind of his own?' There is no way to please her," he lamented.

This friend has not figured out yet that there is no behavior—his or his children's—capable of filling up his mom. She seems to be unfamiliar with the developmental stages of children. If she were, she would know that it is the job of the two-year-old to say no. I don't need to tell that to anyone who has had a two-year-old. It's their job. And it's our job to help them do their job.

HELPING THEM DO THEIR JOB

Whole sets of books have been written on the developmental stages of human beings. The best book I know on the subject is *Self-Esteem: A Family Affair*, by Jean Illsley Clarke.[1] From this greatly abridged treatment of the topic we learn what can be expected from

[1] *Self-Esteem: A Family Affair* (Center City, MN: Hazelden, 1998).

children at various ages and stages. That way we can be careful not to hold a two-year-old accountable for six-year-old behavior, for example. For a more specific understanding of what is normal for your child's age, I refer you to Jean Clarke.

So how can we help them do their job? When a infant cries, she is doing her job. A baby is simply telling us that she has a need. She is learning to get what she needs by asking. Our job is to figure out what the need is and meet it, not to expect silence. When we decode the request and respond, the infant is learning to trust. I don't think it is possible to spoil an infant—and think of how shaming it is to refer to someone as "being spoiled."

When two-year-olds say no, they are finding out that they are separate human beings from their parents, with separate wills and separate opinions. Though most Christian parents have been trained to balk at this concept, it is our job to help them develop a strong *no*. They are going to need a strong *no* when they are fourteen years old and someone wants to be sexually intimate with them, or shoves a bottle of alcohol in their hand. Our job is to recognize opportunities for them to exercise their *no*—not to strip them of their will in the name of maintaining authority as a parent.

I am not suggesting that we allow our children to be disobedient, or to disregard the rules, or to be selfish. But instead of grieving that they are in the "terrible twos," I am simply suggesting that we begin to see our precious child's *no* as a signal that they are entering personhood. In that light, actively look for opportunities to give them practice saying *no*, those times when a *no* would be an appropriate answer. Offer to eat their dessert. Ask them if it would be okay for you to cancel your trip together to the zoo. Or ask them if they would like something for supper that they don't like, and when they say no, don't fix it.

One day a blue-in-the-face Erin, who was four, came into our bedroom and held out her hand. "I touched the fire thing," she croaked.

"Show us," we said, so Erin led us to a plug that was half-pulled out of the wall socket. She had wedged her finger behind it and gotten a shock. She was doing her job—the job of the toddler/explorer—by touching the plug. Our job was to make the environment safe for her to do her job, not to punish her for exploring.

When our eleven-year-old daughter questions the rules, and even breaks them, she is doing her job. She is conducting research to find out if there are things in the world that are dependable, laws on which she can count. Our job is to show her, through our structure and how we respond to her choices, that there are indeed firm rules. It is not our job to try to control her testing. In our family, she can count on being held responsible for her choices. She can count on experiencing consequences to help her learn about life. And she can count on being loved and accepted as a person, even if we may hate her behavior.

It is the job of the eighteen-year-old person to leave home. They begin the learning process around the time they enter their teens. They do this by making plans to sleep over at friends' homes. They do it by finding rides to places without you. Our job is to help them leave. We do that by allowing them to get their driver's permit, and by practicing with them. We do it by encouraging them to find a job, and by handing them more freedom to decide things. It is not our job to get into a tug-of-war aimed at getting them to stay. That will only be more painful for parent and child, both of whom are already scared and confused. I have counseled people who have succeeded in preventing their children from leaving. They have a twenty-six-year-old whom they *wish* would leave, but now is firmly entrenched.

TRAINING THEM TO SUCCEED AT WHO THEY ARE

As we have seen, the work of parenting a two-year-old is different than that of parenting a twelve-year-old. Not only that, but there is different work involved in parenting each individual child, no matter what their age. This job requires noticing the individual identities of your children and helping them live consistently with who they are.

Like her sisters, our youngest daughter, Callie, is very creative.

She likes to write stories, draw pictures, and invent intricate creations from scraps of wood, modeling clay, and just about anything she can get her hands on. Where I grew up, the people in church would have said that Callie was selfish. As a parent I would have been instructed to teach her not to be into "self," but into God. Instead of painting, she should be learning Bible verses and getting ready for the mission field. But Callie doesn't need to be fixed, she's not broken. My job as a parent is not to get her to become someone other than who she is for the Lord. My job is to help Callie become all of the artist God created her to be, so that when people see her art and the freedom and joy with which she creates, they see in our little girl a picture of the very Creator himself.

Callie is also very competent in school. She is constantly getting certificates for cooperating, for excelling, for volunteering, for putting in a little extra. But we have noticed that she rarely does anything to draw attention to her accomplishments. The certificates stay in her schoolbag or disappear. She doesn't brag. Since we have noticed this about her, we know it is our job to catch her succeeding. That way we can remind her of how competent she is and compliment her on her effort. We can also remind her at all times that she is special because of Jesus—even the times when she gets a low grade and feels bad, but doesn't say anything.

Kara, our oldest, did not walk until she was eighteen months old. She was extra careful to never fall down, and you can't learn to walk if you don't allow yourself to fall down. We have noticed that her carefulness has carried through to caution in relationships, and that she has difficulties sometimes in trying new things. Because we know this about her, we can support her in these areas.

What Kara lacked in motor skills she made up for in her vocabulary. She could say quite a bit when she was eight months old, and could understand even more. We eventually had her tested in order for her to be able to enter school early. We did not know how to keep challenging her at home.

Erin showed all the vocabulary skills Kara had—but sometimes did not follow through on our verbal instructions. If we asked her to pick up an item and return it to the shelf, for instance, she would pick it up, leave the room—and disappear. Later in the day we would notice that the item was still not on the shelf. We were concerned, so when she was older we had Erin tested at the same place and the same age as Kara. Baffling: Her test scores were just as high as Kara's. So we asked the counselor about the discrepancy between Erin's behavior and her scores. "Kara could do the task when she was eight months old," Holly said, "Why can't Erin do it when she's four?"

"Simple," replied the counselor. "Erin doesn't care about putting items on shelves."

A light went on: Erin did not care about the jobs we cared about.

"Her tests show that she is highly curious and involved with her world. My guess is that she gets distracted by the texture of the wallpaper on the way to the bedroom," said the counselor, "or by the motion of the leaves blowing in the breeze outside her window. Kara is more task-oriented. Erin is more sensory-oriented."

When it is time to do a task, you can say to a task-oriented child, "Please do the dishes, and when you are finished you can go play." The child will complete the task and go play. If you gave that instruction to a sensory-oriented child, they would never get to go play. And they would feel defeated by the task. You might say, instead, "Please do the dishes for ten minutes. I'll set the timer. When it goes off you can go play for half an hour. Then you can come in and work some more."

Please notice that, at that point in our parenting, we were comparing two children. This is not a helpful, grace-full thing to do. This teaches them to get their value in relation to each other, instead of in spirit.

Then there is what is called a *strong-willed* child. Children usually are slapped with this label because they are stubborn about doing their jobs. The strong-willed person who cooperates with the system becomes a trophy. Besides that, a strong-willed child is simply a four-year-old who has figured out what most kids don't figure out until they are in their teens. That is, "Mom and Dad, you can't control me as much as you thought you could."

Jesi is more this type of person in our family. She wants to know "Why?" She pushes, questions, tests, and pushes some more. In fact, Jesi wants to take control of things. Trying to control her most often ends in an ugly power struggle. Sometimes it's actually a good strategy to give her control, and less tiring as well.

For instance, when she was in first grade her teacher told us during a conference that students were complaining because Jesi was constantly tormenting the student in front of her. "Are you having the students tell Jesi to knock it off?" I asked.

"Oh, I would never embarrass her like that," replied the teacher.

"Well, are you telling her that what she is doing is not acceptable?" I continued.

"Oh no, that would put her in a difficult position," answered the teacher.

"Well, then, how are you handling this?" I asked.

"Every week I just rearrange the seating of the students, without trying to make it obvious that Jesi is causing a problem."

"It seems to me that Jesi is in control, and she is going to have you moving desks around all year," I observed. "She is misbehaving, but you and the other students are suffering the consequences."

"What do you think I should do?" asked the teacher.

"Next time this happens," I began, "tell Jesi that the results of this are completely in her control." Here's the plan I suggested: Jesi could choose to stop acting this way, in which case she could have recess and other special activities with the other students. Or she could choose to keep acting this way, in which case she would have to stay at her desk during recess and miss out on the next activity.

I asked the teacher to reassure Jesi that she was capable of making a wise choice.

"Do you think it will work?" the teacher asked.

"Yes," we replied.

At the next conference the teacher said, "I can hardly believe it. It really worked."

There are some who wish we would fix Jesi and make her be more compliant. Jesi isn't bad or in need of fixing, she's just tenacious. Our job is not to control her and turn her into a more pliable person. Our job is to create an environment in which Jesi can be the best, tenacious, strong-willed person Jesus ever had working for Him!

TEACHING THEM WHO THEY ARE IN CHRIST

If your children are believers, they are a brand-new creation (1 Corinthians 5:17). They have been born, chosen, and adopted into God's family because He loves them so much. Because they have new hearts, they are capable of having beliefs, values, and behaviors that are pleasing to God. Christian children are capable of fighting the fight of faith. That is their job. Our job is to create a grace-full environment in which they can learn to live consistently with their new heart and the Holy Spirit who lives in them.[2]

You can do the best job of helping your children do their job if you know what their job is. Find out. In Proverbs we read:

> There are three things which are too wonderful for me, four which I do not understand: The way of an eagle in the sky, the way of a serpent on a rock, the way of a ship in the middle of the sea, and the way of a man with a maid. (Proverbs 30:18–19)

---

[2] There is a wonderful resource to help parents help their children develop a correct biblical view of selfhood. It is called *Search for Significance, Youth Edition Discussion Manual,* by Dawson McAllister and Robert S. McGee. It can help them untangle incorrect beliefs about self-esteem and where it comes from, and form new beliefs about who they are in Christ. Now out of print, it is available online from many sellers.

It is obvious that the writer has spent enough time watching these things to be amazed by them. I would like to urge all parents to add a fifth item to this list of *wonderful-to-watch* things: the way of each child. Each one is uniquely designed by God. It is only through discovering and building upon who your children are created to be by God that you can help them become all they are destined to be *for* God.

Your first responsibility as a parent is to take care of yourself. A *cared-for* parent who knows how to rest in God is a more adequate resource to family members, and less likely to resort to control and manipulation in an attempt to find satisfaction from the performance of others. Families that are performance-oriented often create environments in which parents and children are *caused to stumble*—that is, they keep failing and eventually want to give up. In chapter 11, we will see what a trap this is, and begin to learn how to escape the trap of control. With this understanding you will be on your way to rebuilding a family that is stronger and freer in spirit.

DISCUSSION QUESTIONS

1. *Proverbs 22:6 is often misinterpreted. Or is there more than one way to look at it? Discuss.*

2. *Why is it important not to stereotype children with regard to their sex?*

3. *Is the concept of training children according to their individual personalities and strengths new for you? Share some examples of how this works.*

4. *Why would treating a child as the individual he is be more freeing than expecting him to do everything just as his older sibling has done?*

11. Equipping Without Tripping

Jesus once made a rather alarming statement—one that Christian parents need to contemplate: "Whoever causes one of these little ones who believe in Me to stumble, it is better for him that a heavy millstone be hung around his neck, and that he be drowned in the depth of the sea" (Matthew 18:6).

In the past, when I heard this passage, I used to picture a jet-black stretch limousine pulling up next to one of my kids. The smoked-glass window comes down. Slowly, a dastardly character pokes his hand out of the dark interior and offers my little one drugs and sex as a way for her to get her needs met. Yes, it is comforting to know that Jesus stands against evil people who want the bodies and souls of our children. It never occurred to me, though, that he might also be talking to me.

If we look more carefully at Matthew 18, we see that Jesus is not talking to drug-pushers and flesh-salesmen—He's talking to His *disciples*. These were people who cared about the things of God and who were being trained to point out to others the right spiritual path to God. Is it possible that Jesus' own followers were in danger of causing others to turn away from Him, to follow empty things as their source of spiritual well-being?

It seems that is exactly what Jesus is warning about. Jesus was talking about causing others to stumble, and addressing himself to people who never dreamed they would do such a thing. This brings us to the fourth principle of "parenting by the Book": *Don't cause the little ones to stumble.* It is my assumption that you are a caring parent whose main concern about your children is that they believe in Jesus and grow up to be healthy adults.

LOOKING AT THE CONTEXT

"Who then is the greatest in the kingdom of heaven?" This is the question the disciples opened their dialogue with—a question about earning points with God. That question was so far off the mark Jesus did not even bother to answer it. Instead, He used a visual aid to give His answer—a four- to seven-year-old child (as indicated by the Greek word used).

No doubt the child looked like any one of ours would have looked at that age: scuffed knees, disheveled clothes, a nose in need of attention, and messy hair.

"Unless you are converted and become like children," Jesus said, "you shall not enter the kingdom of heaven. Whoever then humbles himself as this child, he is the greatest in the kingdom of heaven."

Notice that Jesus did not come anywhere near the performance standards by which the disciples, as first-century Jews, had been trained to live. Instead, He answered the question about how one enters the kingdom at all: Unless you are like this little kid, you don't get in. Then He came back around to the original question, and His answer went something like this: To get in, you have to be like a child. If you're like a child—unpretentious, humble, what-you-see-is-what-you-get—you're the greatest. Therefore, everyone who learns how to live simply by finding life in God is the greatest.

This answer was aimed at the people who were going to be left to do the ministry after Jesus was gone. I think Jesus was concerned that His disciples were preoccupied with earning points in a kingdom where there are no points to earn! That is why He raised the issue about the simple, trusting way we get into the kingdom in the first place—with all our needs in plain view. And I believe Jesus was concerned about those to whom the disciples would carry the message of the kingdom after He was gone. Seeing they were concerned about earning points with God, He didn't want them to cause others to get off on the wrong foot. In fact, if they set new believers out on the wrong path, after they'd entered the kingdom by grace, they would be guilty of causing these little ones to stumble.

WHAT IT MEANS TO "STUMBLE"

A person stumbles when his eyes are focused on one thing and an obstacle is laid at his feet. Notice that Jesus is referring to the "little ones who believe in Me"—who trust in Jesus as their Source. They rely on Him and look to Him for their safety needs, identity, and sense of value. It is easy to see that the person in the black limousine is offering an opportunity to look to something besides Jesus: Looking to drugs or sex to meet your needs, and away from Jesus, will obviously cause those who believe in Him to stumble. But this is not what Jesus is confronting.

I believe that Romans 9 is the best passage from which to gain an understanding of the meaning of the word *stumble*. Here the apostle Paul says, "What shall we say then? That Gentiles, who did not pursue righteousness, attained righteousness, even the righteousness which is by faith; but Israel, pursuing a law of righteousness, did not arrive at that law. Why? Because they did not pursue it by faith, but as though it were by works. They stumbled over the stumbling stone" (vv. 30–32). Can you see it? Stumbling results from pursuing righteousness as though it were obtained by works.

This means that we aren't talking about a black limousine. We're talking about a white limousine with a cross hanging from the mirror and a bumper sticker that says, "Jesus First." Only when the window opens, the voice from within tells us that positive, religious performance is the means of keeping God's approval. Yes, we were offered salvation as a free gift—but now, to keep God happy we need to work for perfect-attendance pins, we need to give enough, and we need to minister. Works become the focus—and people who don't look where they're going *stumble*.

Here, then, is the literal translation of Matthew 18:6:

> Whoever causes one of these little ones who believes in Me to pursue God's approval as though it were by good behaviors, it would be better for that person that the kind of millstone the oxen push [there was also a little household kind] be hung around his neck and he be drowned in the deepest part of the ocean, the part that is the farthest away from land where nobody ever goes.

What does this rendering evoke in us as Christian leaders, and as parents?

A TALE OF TWO FAMILIES

What, then, is the difference between Christian parenting that "causes the little ones to stumble" and the kind that "brings them up in the discipline and instruction of the Lord"? This is another way to contrast parenting that is curse-full with the kind that is grace-full. These two types of parenting look different in many ways, with the major differences falling into three categories: Parenting Goal; Method; Hoped-for Result. This can be seen in the following chart:

Result:	Cause to Stumble	Bring up in the Lord
Parenting Goal:	Create an environment of control.	Create an environment of empowering.
Method:	"Barricading" and punishing.	Surrounding with grace-full relationships
Hoped-for Result:	People who *look* healthy.	People who *are* healthy.

DIFFERENT PARENTING GOALS

Curse-full parenting. The goal of curse-full parents is to control the behavior of their children. You will remember that the main dynamic of the curse is the desire to control, which occurs when one person places him/herself over another. These parents view themselves as being responsible for their children's choices, but not always responsible for their own. In a controlling environment, the end justifies the means. Therefore, it's all right if the parent rages, manipulates, or otherwise acts inappropriately in order to get the desired resulting behavior. They can hit their children to get them to stop hitting each other. They can yell at their children to get them to be quiet. They can call them names so that the children will stop name-calling. And curse-full parents are T.I.R.E.D.

When we as parents are over-responsible for the behavior of our children (and under-responsible for our own behavior as parents), we disempower our children. We prevent them from becoming capable, we enable them to not be responsible for their behavior, and we provoke them to seething hostility. This kind of parenting causes the little ones to stumble because it creates an environment in which the children learn to perform in order to be loved and accepted. Love and acceptance is a gift because of Jesus; it cannot be earned.

Grace-full parenting. The goal of the grace-full parent is to create

141

an environment in which children are empowered. Jesus told the disciples, "You shall receive power when the Holy Spirit has come upon you" (Acts 1:8). As I have already mentioned, the greatest source of power to help people face life's issues is "to allow themselves to be continuously filled with the Spirit." Hence, grace-full parents are constantly looking for opportunities to remind their children to draw life and fulfillment from Jesus alone.

On a flesh-and-blood level, there are other words that communicate the concept of empowering: *serving, equipping, building, preparing, unleashing, training, providing opportunities*—all of these are elements of the kind of parenting that empowers children.

When Kara was in the first grade, she was enrolled in a special class at school. The teacher was supposed to send someone down to get Kara each day, but she often forgot and Kara missed the class. One day, a sad Kara came to Holly and me and said, "I think I'm in trouble. I'm supposed to be in this class, but I've missed it for two weeks. Someone is supposed to come and get me, but they never come."

"Talk to the teacher, Kara—you're capable," we said.

"I'm afraid," she said.

"We want you to talk to her. One of us will come with you to see her—but *you* are doing the talking."

There I was, holding Kara's hand as we went to meet with the teacher after school.

"Hi," I began, "I'm Kara's dad. She has something she needs to say." I looked at her, which was her cue.

She gulped and then told her sad tale.

The teacher apologized, and then told Kara she was glad she had talked to her. Then the woman looked at me. I said, "Thank you. Good-bye."

That was all I said. After all, I wasn't the one who needed to talk to the teacher. On the way home I told Kara she had done a great job, and I pointed out how capable she was. It was Kara's job to talk to her teacher; it was my job to empower her—that is, to lend her enough of my power—so she could do her job.

Empowering is accomplished through training, or the process of discipling—*not* through controlling. A disciple is someone who has learned to do what the master-teacher does. Hopefully, as an adult, I am able to talk to someone when I have an issue with them. My job as a parent is to discipline my daughters to be able to do that job when they have issues of their own. In other words, my main job is to hand my kids their jobs. Parents who empower work hard, but they don't wind up as tired as controlling parents because eventually everyone is prepared and doing their own work.

DIFFERENT METHODS

Curse-full and grace-full families employ different methods to accomplish their goals.

Curse-full parenting. As we've already noted, the main parenting goal in a curse-full family is control. Control is attempted through two primary methods.

The first is what I would call a *barricade* style of parenting. Those who use this approach act as if the problem is the presence of all the outside evil forces in the world. The solution, then, is to control the behavior of the children by building barriers around them—that is, by forbidding them from doing things, going places, being with certain people, listening to certain kinds of music.

Several years ago Minnesota raised the drinking age from eighteen to twenty-one. I agree with this decision. But if the decision was made over concern that our eighteen- to twenty-year-olds were making poor choices, or to ensure that they would make wise choices, then something has not happened in the lives of these people. Is it possible for a healthy, wise nineteen-year-old to be in an unhealthy environment and still make healthy choices? Yes.

Are barricades okay? Yes, at times. But let me illustrate what

143

I learned about the inadequacy of barricades from my daughters. When they were little we had one of those spring-loaded gates that parents use to keep the little ones in or out of a room. "Don't go into the kitchen," we would say to daughters A, B, and C. Daughter A would toddle up to the barricade and no farther. But the truth is, this child would not have gone into the kitchen even without the gate, just because we told her not to. Daughter B would look at us, toddle over to the gate, kick it over, and toddle into the kitchen anyway. This is not cooperation or obedience. Daughter C would toddle up to the gate and then hang as much of her anatomy over the barrier without actually touching it or entering the kitchen, and all the while she would look at us with a wry little smile on her face. It was as if she wanted us to know that she could be in and out of the kitchen both at the same time, but that we couldn't do anything about it because she had escaped on a technicality. (What a legalist!) This is not cooperation or obedience either.

This is to say, barricades work most often for people who don't need them anyway. Yes, parents, it is fine to have wise barriers—but don't put too much stock in them. The problem with our children is not the presence of bad things on the outside. It is the absence of spiritual, emotional, and psychological strength on the inside.

The second method used in a curse-full family is *punishment.* By punishment I do not mean providing or pointing out consequences. When the process of discipline takes place in a grace-full context, consequences are given to enable children to learn about life. They are a way of saying that people are responsible for their own behavior and capable of making appropriate choices. By punishment I mean making people pay for their behaviors as a way to obtain right standing. Punishments are often used to blackmail, coerce, or threaten children into performing the way the parent wants them to. This is control, and it provides occasion for children to become focused on their good behaviors as the means of earning love and acceptance.

Grace-full parenting. Rather than trying to control, grace-full parents provide discipline through which their children learn to make wise choices. The primary method used to accomplish this is to provide a grace-full relationship context. In curse-full relationships, rules and performance take the place of people and needs. In a family that seeks to be a place of grace, relationships are there to make sense of the rules: Interaction is there to make sense of the way we need to perform to be successful at growing in maturity.

A grace-full family is a place where people can do the job of learning to live without the fear of losing love and acceptance if the job gets too messy. In order to get good at anything, you need to practice. That includes the process of learning to live and the mistakes that occur. In grace-full relationships, mistakes are seen as learning opportunities. In curse-full relationships mistakes are seen as opportunities to feel bad about yourself.

Grace-full relationships are also the place in which the training/discipling process can take place. In Philippians, the apostle Paul talks about this in regard to his own learning process. See how easily it applies to the learning we want to occur in our family. Paul says:

> Not that I speak from want; for I have learned to be con-tent in whatever circumstances I am. I know how to get along with humble means, and I also know how to live in prosper-ity; in any and every circumstance I have learned the secret of being filled and going hungry, both of having abundance and suffering need. I can do all things through Him who strength-ens me. (Philippians 4:11)

I want to draw your attention to the two Greek words translated "learned" in English. They are not the same word. One is from the word *mueo* and it means "initiated." The other is *emathon*, a form of the word *mathatais*. Peter, James, and John were *mathatais*, disciples—they had been trained firsthand by Jesus.

How did Paul come to "know" how to overcome all of the things he mentions in this passage? Not from being told; not from reading it in a book; not from hearing a sermon. The words indicate that Paul had been through both an initiation process *and* a process of being discipled. In other words, Paul knew about being hungry and full because he had been hungry and full. He knew about being poor and prosperous because he had been through those experiences. He knew he could be content in any and every circumstance. His success came because he had a relationship with Christ, whose grace gave him the strength to get through.

This is the potential that grace-full relationships have. Through them we can provide a context in which children can learn to be wise decision-makers instead of compliant parent-pleasers. One day we—the barrier-placers, will not be there to place barriers or provide consequences. Will our children be strong, governed, and strengthened from within?

DIFFERENT HOPED-FOR RESULTS

Curse-full parenting. A movie that came out a few years ago was called *Johnny Handsome*—the true story of a man whose face and head were severely deformed. Not only that, but his childhood was one of abuse and neglect. His mother was a prostitute, who visited him infrequently in the state home until she died when he was thirteen. He didn't know who his father was. Full of rage, he hated himself and everyone else. When Johnny left the institution as a young adult, he immediately fell in with a bad crowd. During a robbery attempt he was double-crossed by his partners, who also murdered his best friend. Johnny was captured and sent to prison.

While locked up, a prison doctor took a special interest in him. This surgeon believed that Johnny was basically a good guy, just a victim of circumstances beyond his control. He offered to bring Johnny into an experimental program in which he would perform surgery on Johnny's deformities. Along with giving him a new face, the program would also give him a new name, find him a job, and release him early on parole. The doctor believed that, with all this going for him, Johnny would be on his way to a happy, successful life.

On the sidelines was the police detective who had originally arrested Johnny. He had followed Johnny throughout his career in crime. The detective cautioned the doctor that Johnny was simply using him. He knew Johnny, and did not believe that these external changes would make a difference. Every so often he would pop back into the movie and renew his warning. The doctor discounted him as a doomsayer.

The movie ends with Johnny using his new appearance and pretend identity to trick his former partners into doing another robbery with him. His plan is to double-cross and then kill them. At least he will get revenge on them for double-crossing him and for killing his best friend. Tragically, the attempt fails, and though Johnny is able to shoot his enemies he is also fatally shot. The police detective arrives on the scene, looks at the dying Johnny, and says, "The doctor didn't understand this part."

Curse-full parents don't understand this part either: Growing from being an empty, incompetent baby to a full, competent adult is like walking a tightrope—a long, hard, scary process, both for parents and for kids. In these families, the children's performance is not only their sole source of validation, it is the means by which the parents feel validated. Everyone earns love, value, and acceptance on the basis of the child's performance. The hoped-for result is this: people who look healthy, whether they are or not.

Parenting that focuses on a child's external performance as the most important thing causes the little ones to stumble and fail to benefit from the grace offered in Jesus.

Grace-full parenting. What was it the doctor missed? He did not grasp the truth that *full-looking-but-empty* people are still *empty*. We need to understand this as Christian parents. What we want from our parenting efforts is a person who knows how to live in a healthy way. We know the process of living honestly is dangerous and messy. Yes, we and our children will make mistakes, and may even look stupid. But as our children try to be successful at this tricky business of life, we provide a net of grace to catch them—for they will fall. That means love, acceptance, and value are given to everyone on the basis of Christ's finished work on the cross.

What a great net grace is. It makes it safe to try. The family that offers grace sends a message that failure is not the end of the story.

Yes, there are a lot of dangers out there—a lot of folks in black limousines. We need to warn our children about them and protect our children from them. But let's raise children who are full of real life on the inside.

DISCUSSION QUESTIONS

1. *Who was Jesus speaking to when He said, "Whoever causes one of these little ones to stumble . . ."? Who was He speaking about?*

2. *Who do we have to become in order to get into the kingdom of heaven? Why do you think Jesus used this example?*

3. *What does it mean to "stumble" in the context of Jesus' teaching in Matthew 18:6?*

4. *Describe the difference between curse-full parenting and grace-full parenting.*

5. *What did you take away from the true story of the boy with deformed facial features who was restored by the compassionate doctor?*

PART III

Families Where Grace Is in Place

Introduction

As we have established, trying to control others is both the root and the fruit of the curse as it works its way in our relationships. Learning how to allow the Holy Spirit to empower us from within is the key to having grace-full families. When the adults know they are loved and accepted by God, they do not have to try to draw fulfillment from the good performance of their children.

Now I want to approach this from a slightly different angle: As adults, we are responsible for ourselves, to live in ways that are consistent with the grace we've received and who we are in Christ. We know that people in God's kingdom are not devalued for having problems; if we are stuck, we can get help. We also know we are responsible to be resources through whom God shows family members grace and equips them to live. In this part of the book, we will draw all that we've learned so far into a cohesive picture, showing what it means to be members of families where grace is in place.

12. A Grace-Full Family

For several years after graduation from seminary, I worked at a human-services agency. All employees were required to obtain a certain amount of outside training each year. One of the training experiences in which I participated was most stretching, and threatening.

I had enrolled in a workshop that had to do with building self-esteem. It met for eight weeks, two hours a night.

I'll never forget that first night. The workshop leader outlined the topics to be covered in the eight weeks ahead: *Nurturing, Feelings, Affirmation, Role-Playing, Negative Strokes,* and *Warm Fuzzies.* You should know I was the only male in a class of twenty-six. My anxiety level was off the charts.

All kidding aside, this seminar turned out to be one of the most significant, life-changing experiences I've ever had. But there was the one source of discomfort I couldn't get past: the fact that I was the only male; it was a nightmare. I never felt I belonged. I never felt like I nurtured, role-played, or warm-fuzzied good enough. I never felt happy to be there. In fact, I never knew how I felt—except for one feeling: I hated being the only male in the workshop. Eventually, I even began to feel sad that I was a man at all.

On the last night, the leader said she wanted to close the class by giving each of the participants an affirmation. She went around the room, drawing positive attention to people for their smile, enthusiasm, sense of humor, energy, and a whole list of other things. After each comment, she told each woman how much she had enjoyed being able to spend the eight weeks with her. Then she came to me.

"I'm glad you're a man," she said. It blew me away. All I could do was stare at her. I couldn't believe she said that. *Glad that I was a man?* For eight weeks I had wished I could just disappear. I had felt like my "man-ness" was a liability, a birth defect. Now here was this woman—the chief executive of the workshop, a respected expert on human beings—and she was glad I was a man. Suddenly I was glad I was a man too.

I have thought a lot about what happened during those eight weeks, and especially on that night. The workshop was full of teaching and experiences from which we could *assume* things about being specially created as human beings. But the leader did not leave it up to assumption—she made her point with each of us out loud. And how powerful her words were! What she said went straight into my heart and has stayed there to this day. What she said cast a new light over the entire eight weeks; it transformed an experience I was ready to trash into one that was life-transforming. I don't know if this woman was a Christian or not, but she gave me grace.

Grace-full words are powerful. Relationships in which there is a pervading atmosphere of grace are more powerful still.

GRACE AND SHAME ARE OPPOSITES

In an earlier book I included a chapter entitled "When Shame Is the Name of the Game."[1] The purpose of that chapter was to describe ten characteristics in order to help the reader spot a *shame-based family system*. This is a family system in which members are given constant messages about themselves that something is wrong with them. Love is conditional, based on performance; acceptance as a person is not free, it is earned by performing certain behaviors and avoiding others. Even under the best circumstances, then, *people* are not loved and accepted; *behavior* is all-important.

It is not surprising that a grace-full family looks entirely different than a shame-based family. As a matter of fact, it is the opposite. Therefore, I would like to use those characteristics found in shame-based relationships as a springboard from which to step into a discussion on the characteristics of a grace-full family.

In shame-based relationships you will find the following characteristics:

1. Out-loud shaming. The message communicated is: "Something is wrong with you"; "You are defective"; "You don't measure up"; "Why can't you be like . . ."
2. Performance-orientation. The focus is on doing certain good behaviors and avoiding others as a means of earning love, gaining acceptance, acquiring approval, or proving value. Failure to perform results in shame.
3. Unspoken rules. Behavior is governed by rules or standards that are seldom, if ever, spoken out loud. In fact, sometimes the only way they are discovered is when they are broken. There is a "can't-talk-about-it" rule in effect—which means no one is supposed to notice or mention problems; and if you speak out about a problem, you are the problem. This forces people to

---

[1] *Tired of Trying to Measure Up* (Minneapolis: Bethany House), 1990.

keep quiet. There is also a "can't-win" rule in effect. For instance, children are taught never to lie; they are also told to never tell Grandma her meatloaf tastes bad. No matter how hard you try to keep these contradictory rules, you always fail to perform. And failure to perform results in shame. These rules tend to govern future relationships, unless they are realized and intentionally renounced.

4. Communicating through "coding." Talking about feelings or needs leaves you feeling ashamed for being so "selfish." Talking about problems breaks the "can't-talk-about-it" rule and gets you shamed for being the problem. Therefore, family members learn to say things in code, or they send messages to each other indirectly through other people.

5. Idolatry. Family members are taught to turn to things and people other than God's acceptance as the measure of their value and identity. The measuring stick becomes: how things look; what people think; religious behavior; acquiring possessions.

6. Putting kids through a hard time. Kids are involved in the messy and imperfect process of finding out about life. But the family cares most about how things look and what people think. Therefore, just being a kid becomes a shaming thing. Children must learn to act like miniature adults in order to avoid shame.

7. Preoccupation with fault and blame. Since there is such a focus on performance in this family, lack of performance must be tracked down and eradicated. Fault and blame are the order of the day. The purpose of the question, "Who is responsible?" is to find out who is to blame. That way the culprit can be shamed, humiliated, and made to feel so bad that he won't do the behavior again.

8. Strong on "head skills." Family members become experts at defending themselves. Blaming, rationalizing, minimizing, and denial are just some of the ways people try to push away the shame message—usually in vain.

9. Weak on "heart skills." "Can't-feel" is another rule governing this system. Feelings are wrong, selfish, or unnecessary. People in shame-based families don't know how they feel or how to respond to their feelings. These are emotionally reactive places.

10. Needy people. Because love and acceptance was earned on the basis of behavior, but never received apart from performance, shame-based families are characterized by members who are empty on the inside, full-looking on the outside.

WHAT IS A GRACE-FULL FAMILY?

By God's design, the primary channel for learning one's identity, for having needs met, for understanding who God is, and for developing relationships—is the family. Relationships, especially those in families, are powerful. In families we can acquire a deeply ingrained sense of defectiveness and never measuring up—or we can develop the inner strength and outside skills to fully function as healthy human beings.

As I said earlier, grace-full relationships function in ways that are totally opposite of those that are shame-based. In a grace-full family, church, or group, individuals receive messages that they are loved and accepted, valuable, and not alone to face life. The following is a list of ten characteristics that best describe those grace-full relationships from which competent, creative, contented people emerge:

1. *Out-loud affirming* (vs. out-loud shaming). Hearing is one of the senses through which people receive information about themselves, others, and life. Ears are not equipped with tiny filters that only let in wholesome messages of support. *Every* message gets in. As adults we can learn to consciously push away certain messages that shame us and tear us down. But the fact that we have to do so

much work to reject those messages means we have heard them loud and clear in the first place.

In grace-full families, members are told they are loved and accepted, capable, valuable, and supported *out loud*. Don't expect people to be mind readers: It is not realistic to think that they "just know" that you care. Phrases like "I love you," "You are so capable," "I'm here for you when you need me," "I'm glad God put you in our family," "I'm glad you're a boy/girl," "I feel good when I'm with you," and using a person's name when speaking to him are just some of the out-loud ways to affirm people.

My daughters live in a world where in most places—including church—women receive shaming messages because they are women. Both Holly and I decided to equip our girls to compensate for that, starting when they were just babies: We whispered, "I'm glad you're a girl," "I like holding you," "You are so special." And we still affirm them to this day.

2. *People-oriented* (vs. performance-oriented). David Seamands says, "We all need an environment where we feel our needs are met because of who we are and not because of what we do."[2] In grace-full families, love and acceptance does not fluctuate depending on how people act. People are affirmed for being who they are. In shame-based families, behavior is the most important thing. Who you are comes in last.

Members of grace-full families separate people from their behavior. You as a parent can learn to send people-approving messages, even in the midst of unacceptable behavior. Then you will have accomplished what is the hardest, yet most significant work of relationships. I don't like what Holly and the girls do at times, but as far as I'm concerned, they are pre-approved and their worth is not up for grabs.

For example, let's say that one daughter is hitting another. I

[2] *Healing Grace* (Wheaton, IL: Victor Books, 1988).

might say to her, "I don't like how you are acting." This is about her behavior. If she acts hurt by what I said, or hangs her head like she is some second-class citizen, she may have interpreted my message to mean I don't like *her*. At that point, I would clarify by saying, "[name], I like you. That will never change. But right now I don't like how you are treating your sister."

This dynamic exists in our relationship with God as well. We have a relationship with God because He loves us and thinks we were worth dying for, and not because we behaved well enough to deserve it. Paul says, "But God demonstrates His own love toward us, in that while we were yet sinners, Christ died for us" (Romans 5:8). God hates how we live sometimes (our behavior), but "there is therefore now no condemnation for those [people] who are in Christ Jesus" (Romans 8:1).

3. *Out-loud rules and expectations* (vs. unspoken rules). In a grace-full family, rules are there to serve people; people are not there to serve the rules. In order for rules to serve the family most effectively, everyone needs to know what the rules are. If a rule favors certain people (the adults, an older child, the baby of the family), or is too rigid or silly to say out loud, you should not have that rule. And it is not okay to hold people accountable for rules they did not verbally know were in operation.

Some families have an unspoken rule that says, "Adults are more important than children." If you want to have a rule that says, "Adults and children are *equally* important," then neither adults nor children should be allowed to interrupt when someone else is talking.

In shame-based families, the person who says there is a problem becomes the problem. In a grace-full family, the truth spoken or revealed is never the problem, nor is the person who speaks it. The problem is dealt with as a real problem, and a solution is sought. And because people don't lose points for having problems or failing to perform, you can even talk about it.

Try this sometime: Sit down with your family for an hour and let everyone talk about the rules they think are in place. Then let them also talk about the rules they think should be in place. I think you will find this to be a very enlightening experience.

4. *Communication is clear and straight* (vs. coding). Zechariah 8:16 says:

> "These are the things which you should do: Speak the truth to one another; judge with truth and . . . let none of you devise evil in your heart against another, and do not love perjury; for all these things are what I hate," declares the Lord.

Can you see what God thinks about telling the truth?

If you want someone to take out the garbage, ask them to do so. Don't say, "Sure would be nice if someone would take out the garbage," and then complain when people ignore or miss your coded message. If you'd rather have hamburgers than hot dogs, say so. Don't say, "I don't care, we can have whatever you want," and then pout when you end up with hot dogs. If you need help, ask for it. Don't say, "No, it's no big deal. I'll be fine," and then feel sorry for yourself or judge others as inconsiderate if no one helps you.

Coding isn't helpful for anyone—least of all for children. Kids are very literal. Alfred Adler noted that children are great *observers* but terrible *interpreters*. People receiving your messages should not have to decode them. When you want to send a message, decode it first yourself and then send it straight. (You'll find out a lot about yourself!)

Don't *triangle*—that is, do not get in the middle of other people's relationships and run messages. I have found that the reason people run messages for their family members is so those members will be able to get along. The irony is that by running messages you are ensuring that they never have to get along on their own. Set an internal boundary, and do not let people tell you things they need to tell someone else. If those involved end up with a poor relationship, it will be because they did not do the work it takes to have a good one. Stepping in to "fix" things and "decoding" are not your job, nor is it your job to get people to talk to each other. When you do so, you are only controlling. Your job is to support each of the quibblers in talking to each other. They control what happens after that. Their relationship is their job.

Paul says, "Therefore, laying aside falsehood, speak truth, each one of you, with his neighbor, for we are members of one another" (Ephesians 4:25). *Do what this Scripture says.* Say what you have to say. Expect others to do it, and then don't participate in the outworking of it if they won't.

5. *God is the Source* (vs. idolatry). As Christians, God is our Source. He is our *need-meeter,* our *vindicator,* our *defender,* the *one who has the last word on our value and acceptance.* We are not valuable and acceptable because of how much money we make, the clothes we wear, our church attendance, or because we have been faithful in our giving. Other people can think whatever they want—and they will. What they say might feel hurtful sometimes—but they do not decide the truth about us, God does.

In grace-full families it's okay to be concerned, for instance, about the children's grades. But good grades do not make people more acceptable—just as poor grades do not make them less acceptable. People are acceptable and valuable because of God's love and grace toward them. And they need help remembering that even as you help them improve their grades.

The reason why having faith is such a fight (1 Timothy 6:12) is because we have a Source we *cannot see.* Right now we live among people and are surrounded by things we *can see.* Therefore, it is a fight to keep drawing our sense of value and acceptance from this unseen Source while most of what we see and hear demands that we measure up to someone's external standard in order to be acceptable. In this fight we will sometimes experience hurt feelings because of the words spoken about us or the actions of others. And sometimes we will not know how to act appropriately ourselves. But grace-full families and churches are our most important allies in this battle. In supportive relationships, members are pointed toward God's grace, not toward their performance or how things look or what people think. God is always our only source of hope.

6. *Children are enjoyed* (vs. giving the kids a hard time). In shame-based families, children must act like little adults in order to keep from being shamed. In grace-full families it's okay for them to act like kids. That is why in an earlier chapter I emphasized the need to know about developmental stages. Normal, healthy kids are "messy" about this business of growing up. As a parent, you do not need to be threatened or take it personally when your children mess up. They aren't broken; you don't have to fix them. They are simply exploring life, constantly engrossed in the process of finding out what's real. That's why many children ask so many questions. *Answer their questions.*

When they were little, our kids had a children's book about a bear named Timothy. In one part of the book Timothy was supposed to eat his peas. He hated peas so he hid them under his plate. His mom found them and said, "Timothy, eat your peas." Then he hid them in his napkin. Again, his mother found them and said, "Timothy, eat your peas." Next, he flicked them across the room. His mother caught him and said, "Timothy, eat your peas." Finally he resigned himself to eating them, to a rousing chorus of "Little Green Balls of Mushy Poison." To which his mother replied, "Timothy, act your age!" You had to turn the page to see Timothy's response, and a brilliant response it was. "But Mom, I'm only four," he pleaded.

What simple wisdom! The next time you feel the urge to tell your children to act their age, pay attention. They probably are.

Paying attention to your kids and their struggles can have an added benefit most parents miss: It will give you a chance to rework or finish some things you may have missed out on when you were a kid. You may be able to discover a part of you that you had taken from you when you were young. This is like a lost treasure refound. Don't miss it when God gives you this second chance.

7. *Responsibility and accountability* (vs. fault and blame). Fault and blame are used in shame-based families to punish children for their lack of performance. They become tools in the process of trying to control the behavior of others. But people *are* responsible for their choices, and it is appropriate to hold them accountable for them. This is how we learn.

Where do we find the balance? Let me give you an example. Let's say one of my daughters is careless and breaks something—and she's not talking. The fact that she is hiding what she did tells me that she feels guilty about it. She may even wonder if I am going to shame and criticize her if I find out. There are two reasons why I want to know the truth.

First, so I can discipline her. *This does not mean punish.* It means to help her learn something from the incident. This might occur through consequences she receives, or it might happen just by talking together. The second reason I want her to confess is so that I can forgive her. In not talking about what she did, she is carrying the weight of it. If she would just tell me, I could help lift that spiritual weight of guilt from her by offering her forgiveness. I could also see this as an opportunity to remind her that I love her, even though I don't like what she did. Isn't that the purpose of confession in the New Testament? "If we confess our sins, He is faithful and righteous to forgive us our sins and to cleanse us" (1 John 1:9). In many families, confessing to something gets you shamed, blamed, exposed, and humiliated. Not so in families where grace is in place.

8. *"Head skills" are used for learning* (vs. "head skills" used for defending). The human brain is an incredible instrument. And as the old adage goes, "Two heads are better than one." How hopeful and useful it is if that awesome resource is pooled with that of family members and used to learn how to live faithfully and responsibly. In grace-full families, *thinking* is used for the purpose of learning. In

shame-based families it is used to defend, to blame, to make excuses, and to get out of being responsible. All of this mental-dodging to keep from being shamed. What a tragic waste.

In shame-based families, the question "Why did you do that?" is a trap. There is no answer that is acceptable. Whatever you say will be analyzed and criticized. In grace-full families people are pre-approved, and the question "Why did you do that?" is just a simple inquiry to understand the reason why something was done. If the reasoning is faulty and can be changed, the behavior will change as well.

9. *Feelings are valid and useful* (vs. weak on "heart skills"). Feelings are not right or wrong, they simply exist. They are emotional and physiological signals that tell us that something is going on between us and the world around us. The *choices* we make in response to our feelings determine good or bad, right or wrong results of our feelings—that is, whether they are helpful or damaging. Grace-full families recognize the feeling and expression of emotions as opportunities for family members to connect with one another, to complete unfinished relational business, or to support one another in making wise choices in response to how we feel.

10. *It's OK for outsides to match insides* (vs. empty people learning to act full). In grace-full families, what is *real* is more important than how things *look*. Having a safe, unconditionally accepting place where outsides can match insides is really the only way to find out if there are inside needs and problems that must be addressed. Life is seen with a *process* perspective rather than an *event* perspective. This means that people don't have to react, or attempt to "cure" behavior forever. Because God is involved, you don't have to panic: The story is not over, even if it doesn't look too good right now. Unacceptable behaviors are about poor choices, not about our value and acceptance as people. Because that is true, grace-full family members don't have to fix one another in order to fix themselves.

Do not shame yourself if your family has not exhibited these characteristics. You can start now. And you don't have to overwhelm yourself by taking on the entire list and changing by next month. You can pick one or two things to work on for now. Because of God's grace, you have all the time you need. You are capable. You can do it. With these characteristics in mind, let's press on to chapters 13 and 14 for some practical advice about marriage and parenting.

DISCUSSION QUESTIONS

1. *Give an example of grace-full words that have been said to you recently.*

2. *Describe some characteristics of shame-based relationships.*

3. *Describe some characteristics of a grace-full family.*

4. *Why is it important to have rules in a family that are known and understood by every member?*

5. *How is responsibility and accountability different from shaming and blaming?*

6. *How does having God in our lives change the way we look at "fixing others" as a way to fix ourselves?*

13. The Grace-Full Spouse

Many years ago we started a small nonprofit organization. One day I was meeting with an accountant to go over our books and I noticed a column labeled "Suspense."

"What in the world does that mean?" I asked. "And how does the IRS feel about the concept of suspense?"

He laughed and said, "The suspense column is just a reminder to me that there are some items that still need attention—loose ends that need to be tied up. When they are, I sort them into the appropriate categories."

This chapter and the next are the "suspense" chapters. In them I want to tie up loose ends concerning marriage and parenting, and help you see how grace works in real life. No doubt, bringing in the grace perspective can leave you with the need to sort new insights into the appropriate areas of your relationships. Please consider these final perspectives on marriage:

HAVING THE RIGHT "JOB DESCRIPTION"

A few years ago, Holly and I were asked to speak at a family camp on the West Coast. While I was speaking, Holly worked with the kids in the areas of music and drama. During my sessions, I presented concepts and approaches similar to those contained in this book.

As the week went on, I observed various reactions to my material. It seems that many Christians think *authority* is to be used to control others. So you can imagine the confusion, frustration, even anger on the part of people who have spent a lifetime either using domination, manipulation, and similar methods to enforce their rules or having experienced the effect of this kind of domination. And imagine the amazement of those who thought *submission* meant relegating yourself to a nonperson status. Or the sense of freedom at receiving permission to be real and to have needs! Picture the hornet's nest that got stirred up and the discussions that occurred when these folks went back to their cabins at the end of the day—some of which I heard about later.

Some people were angry. But what I noticed most was this: A large number of people seemed to be very uncomfortable and unsettled; the majority, in fact, were reeling from the impact of the material presented. I decided to investigate.

I discovered that a great many of those at the camp were from one particular church. The pastor of that church had come upon a book on Christian marriage with which he strongly agreed. So he arranged for over a hundred copies to be distributed among the married couples in his church. And it seems that what I had been teaching all week strongly contradicted the material in which these people had been immersed for some time.

Here are a few of the ideas the book suggests: Husbands and wives are responsible for meeting each others' needs. The primary need of the wife is affection; the primary need of the husband is sex.

Problems in marriage are the result of each spouse failing to meet these and other needs of the other. It follows then, that solving marriage problems results from each person trying harder and eventually performing well enough to meet all the needs of the other.

This kind of teaching flows out of "curse-full" thinking. In my opinion, it produces people who are controlling, and who become tired from having to do a job that really belongs to our Source.

People at the camp began to understand this. As they did, they realized that tiredness and a sense of not measuring up would always result from the way they'd been taught to live. Some began to say, openly, that they'd been given the wrong job description. They began to rejoice in the fact that they really were acceptable to God, not on the basis of their own performance or that of their spouse. And they were able to begin rejecting the shame they were experiencing for not being or having a "good enough" spouse. This kind of understanding sets a person free to be a *resource* and a *servant*, not a source and a fixer.

RESOURCES, FROM THE SOURCE

Life, value, and meaning are only available as gifts as a result of God's performance in Christ. It is the job of members in a Christian family or church to be resources to one another. As gifts to one another from God, we can have grace-full relationships in which people are served, built up, equipped, and set free. We can remind one another what is *true* about us because of the love and activity of God, our one Source.

Obviously, believing that we or others are responsible for meeting needs will prevent us from being the resources we could be. But sometimes there are other factors.

Are there wounds from past relationships that get in the way of present relationships? If this is true, we need to take the responsibility to get help and support in order to heal so that our pain does not spill over and wound those around us. Have your models for family life been controlling or self-serving? Then become sensitive to relationship issues, and ask people whose relationships you admire if you can observe how they operate.

Is it simply a matter of not knowing the ingredients of healthy relationships? Ask and keep asking until you get clear answers. We are all capable of learning, growing, and changing.

Always remember this: Under the best circumstances, the most healthy, most sensitive, most educated person is still not capable of meeting the needs of another. That is God's responsibility.

LEAVING AND CLEAVING

In chapter 1, we noted that the first two chapters of Genesis present marriage as a "becoming-one-flesh" relationship. In fact, Genesis 2:24 indicates that it is imperative that we "leave and cleave" in order to build this relationship, a truth reiterated by Paul in Ephesians 5.

What does it mean to leave and cleave?

The word translated *cleave* means "to cling," or "stick to," like glue. The ability to do this with your spouse is determined by the degree to which you have left your parents. *Webster's Dictionary* says that *leave* means to "depart or go away from" on the positive side, and "abandon or desert" on the negative side. But we know this is not always easy.

Under normal circumstances, when an unmarried person is in a dependent relationship with his/her parents, a primary relationship exists between them. (I am using the word *dependent* now as you might on your income tax return rather than in reference to some kind of emotional weakness.) When a son or daughter grows up and begins a relationship with the person he/she is going to marry, the relationship with his/her parents is supplemented by another, new, secondary relationship. This can be seen in the following diagram:

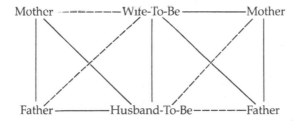

The solid lines represent primary relationships. The broken lines represent secondary relationships. Notice that each person also acquires secondary relationships with the family members of their spouse-to-be.

When they get married, however, things change drastically. Their relationships with the spouse's family members remain the same. But their relationship with their own family members becomes secondary. It might be a different degree of secondary than the relationship with their in-laws, but it is secondary nonetheless. And their relationship with each other becomes primary. It looks like this:

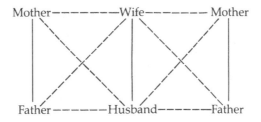

On the surface, leaving implies some kind of geographical change. And it does mean that. In years of counseling married couples, however, I have seen people who have gone away from, departed, even abandoned or deserted their mother and father, *but did not ever really leave*. In other words, they may be present with their spouse, but they are stuck to their parents. This is because they have not really left emotionally, socially, psychologically, or financially. Their allegiance and energy is toward their family of origin and not toward their spouse. This always sends shaming messages to the spouse.

Sometimes in-laws make the situation worse, albeit unintentionally at times. They offer help that bails the couple out of every jam instead of offering to encourage them as they grow through it. They offer unwelcome advice and act hurt or insulted if it's not taken. Or efforts by the new couple to leave and cleave are taken as rejection. These parents control instead of support. It's hard to leave your parents if doing so means you are a "bad child."

One point of clarification: *I am not telling you to break off your relationship with your parents.* I am not saying that you should never socialize with your parents or accept help or support from them. But I am encouraging you to do what it takes to leave your father and mother and cleave to your spouse. You need to do so, whether or not your parents take it personally.

CODEPENDENCY

On a recent talk show, I heard a man who had the dream of becoming a professional athlete in a certain sport. He spent up to eight hours a day, six days a week, playing that sport. He had no job. He had no real marriage. His relationship with his kids was non-existent. The family was in danger of losing the house and all of their possessions. Audience members accused him of lacking respect for his family. He was appalled. He just liked to play his sport.

Members of the audience also accused him of preferring to play rather than work. He admitted it. He just wanted to play. As far as he was concerned, if he could just play six days a week without having to listen to the gripes of his family, life would be just fine.

This scenario recalled for me a book I'd read entitled *The Peter Pan Syndrome.*[1] It was written to help women who thought they

---

[1] Dan Kiley (London: Corgi, 1984).

had married a man, when really they had married a "Pan." You will recall that Peter Pan and the lost boys lived in Never Never Land, where no one ever had to grow up. They just played all day long, going from one incredible adventure to another. The gentleman on the show was very much like a lost boy.

As incredibly out of touch as this man was, my attention was drawn to his wife. While she hated his lifestyle, she funded it. She believed him when he said he respected her, even though all of his actions communicated blatant disrespect. Where he fell short, she took up the slack. Why was she willing to waste her entire life playing "Wendy" to the "Peter Pan" in her husband? She was obviously the smartest, most capable of the two. Yet she lived as if she had no life without him. Why? Because she was a codependent—that is, stuck in a controlling, rescuing relationship that was wearing her out. And the model she provided for her kids, about how to have an adult relationship, was every bit as *dysfunctional* as that of her husband.

As I said earlier, *codependency* is another word for relationship dependency. At its very core, it is a spiritual idolatry. Remember, idolatry occurs when one person turns to anything or anyone besides God in order to gain life, security, and value. In a codependent relationship, God is not the source. Pat Springle, Senior Vice-President of Rapha Hospital Treatment Centers, defines codependency as "a compulsion to control and rescue people by fixing their problems." The codependent needs the loved one to be "fixed" in order to feel good about themselves or as an attempt to have their own unmet needs satisfied.

It is never your job or mine to protect our loved ones from bad news. We can, instead, support them as they learn to cope with the tough challenges of life. We do not have to sacrifice our own needs, feelings, or values as we try to help others with theirs. We can take care of ourselves and be resources to our loved ones as they learn to be responsible for their own needs. You don't have to live in ways that are codependent. If you are not able to stop, get help. Living this way will enable those around you to stay sick or irresponsible.

SUBMISSION

Recently I counseled with a couple who verbalized strong support for the teaching that the husband is the head (the boss), and the wife is to be submissive (to serve the husband's needs and to do what she is told). In real life, the husband was very passive while the wife was controlling. This presented the wife with the strenuous task of *controlling while looking passive.* And the husband had to be *passive while looking like he was the spiritual leader.* This results in a dynamic that I have termed, "the neck that turns the head." It is not headship, and it certainly is not submission.

Pretending to go along with things on the outside that you don't support on the inside is not submission, nor is it humility. It is dishonesty—and probably a spiritualized sugar-coating over seething anger as well. Giving up your own dreams, your ideas, and even your identity in order to earn the approval of another is not submission, nor is it real spirituality. It is a tragedy. Living this way will make you sick.

SEXUALITY

A while ago I flipped through a joke book that made fun of men for being men. It was aggressively degrading, even angry in its tone. I have noticed a similar theme in the comedy of TV shows and comedians. This is wrong.

I heard a well-known Christian preacher on the radio who told the following joke: "In the beginning God created man and the beasts of the field. And God rested. Then he created woman—and man, the beasts, and God have not been able to rest ever since." This is not funny either. It is degrading.

It seems to me that in the context of the history of male/female relationships, it has been a much more common occurrence for men to treat women in a degrading way. We have made fun of them for having feelings, for having menstrual cycles, for being creative. They have been the brunt of our sexual jokes, innuendoes, and harassment, and the victims of our sexually aggressive behavior. Countless Christian books and sermons have echoed Adam's claim that women are to blame for sin in the world. And we have misused God's Word to promote a distorted view of headship and submission. This is wrong.

In Genesis 3:15, God said that He would "put enmity between" the serpent and the woman. The word *enmity* means absolute hatred and open hostility. My belief is that this has resulted in women being a special target of the evil one ever since. I must confess that I have never felt the need to be afraid that I would be the victim of sexual violence while parking my car in a dark lot. Nor have I ever been told that I can't teach a Sunday school class or serve Communion because I am a man. What a tragedy that even Christian men support this hostility toward the daughters of Eve.

SEX

There are many Christian books and teachings like the book I mentioned at the beginning of this chapter. Among other things, such thinking teaches married people how to be codependent (relationship dependent). In fact, it elevates codependency to the status of a virtue. Just as sad, I believe such teachings present a distorted view of sex. I don't believe that sex is the most important need of the male. Consider this. Studies on sexual addiction point out that one of the unhealthy core beliefs of sexual addicts is that "sex is the male's primary need." If "secular" experts are concluding that this thinking is faulty and unhealthy, why are Christians promoting it?

In fact, I don't believe sex is a *need* at all.

If *needs* go unmet long enough, you get sick or die. Nourishment is a need; and hunger is the drive that results ideally in eating food, which meets the need for nourishment. Intimacy is a need, not sex. The sex drive ideally results in sexual activity, which is one way the need for intimacy is met. In fact, while there are many ways to be intimate—and women tend to know more of these than men—sex seems to be the most intimate way God has provided to be intimate. (That is why inappropriate sexual behavior before or after marriage causes people such deep and long-lasting pain.) But you will not get sick or die without sex, despite attempts to tell you otherwise.

COMMUNICATION

Not long ago a man was sitting in my office, describing the frustration he felt in trying to communicate with his wife. He asked, "Have you ever seen one of those bug zappers with the blue lights in them?"

"Sure."

"That's what it's like," he said, "when my wife and I try to talk to each other. It seems that we are so easily hurt and so ready to be defensive, we can't even have a conversation. So what she says gets zapped before I ever really hear it. And the same thing happens with what I say."

This brings me to a final issue: the need for healthy communication in a marriage. I don't simply mean that people should talk more, though it is true that most couples *should* talk more. But for communication to be healthy, it needs to be *purposeful*. Many people need to learn how to say "on purpose" what they really mean, and to stop saying what they don't mean. And they must think about what it is they are hearing and what it really means. Otherwise they may simply spend more time talking, but not hearing or being heard.

My Hardest Struggle

I must confess that speaking and hearing "on purpose" has been the hardest thing for me in our marriage. And it's not just because I'm a man. Like many people, I come from a family background where people did not say what they really meant. Things were said in code, and words were used to control. Therefore, I received no training in saying what I mean. I learned to control, not just communicate. And I learned to speak and hear *crookedly* as well. Let me illustrate what I mean by crooked speaking and crooked hearing.

Several years ago, an excited Holly told me that she wanted to audition for an event that was taking place in our area. It sounded like it was right up her alley, and I encouraged her to go for it. As the deadline approached, I noticed that she hadn't auditioned yet. I felt concerned because I knew this was important to her—and for some reason she was procrastinating. On a previous occasion, she had not auditioned and felt disappointed after the deadline had passed. I wanted to communicate my support to her. I could have done that by saying something like, "Holly, are you still planning to audition, or have you changed your mind? You know, you're capable of doing a great audition. Is there something I can do to help?"

Instead I said, "Are you going to audition, or are you going to let this one slip by too?" It was designed to be a verbal kick in the pants. I had made it my job to get her to audition, and used shaming words. Instead of just saying what I meant, I was trying to control the results.

I have also had to learn to straighten out my crooked hearing. When we moved into the house with the sauna, a lot of painting and decorating needed to be done. We knew a young guy in our church youth group who needed some work for the summer, so we decided that we'd have him paint the living room. He'd never painted before, but there was a lot to do and he needed the money. The room had vaulted ceilings, and this was not a job for a rookie. I told myself this was a "ministry" to him—but I was skeptical.

He took about two days to trim and roll the room. He finished late the second night, so we paid him and he left. A few mistakes were evident, but basically it looked like he'd done a good job. We went to bed with the feeling that everybody made out pretty well on this deal.

The light of the next morning told a different tale. When rolling the brown paint onto the wall, our painter had periodically tilted the roller at the top. Consequently, there was a small brown oval about every two feet apart around the entire perimeter of the white sprayed ceiling. It looked as if a tiny space creature with a very long stride had walked around our ceiling in gravity boots.

I decided to get up very early the next morning and paint the dining room myself. I was almost finished when Holly got up and walked into the room. As I rolled my way to artistic greatness, she noticed something that I did not see yet: That same little alien who had been in the living room had evidently been walking around in the dining room as well. "You're as goofy a painter as George," she chuckled.

Holly was kidding. But inwardly I heard what she said differently, and I reacted. I seethed in silence: *Who needs this! This is the last painting I'm doing around here if I'm just going to be criticized. She can do the painting from now on!*

Fortunately, I noticed what I was thinking and I noticed that, in mid-brush-stroke, our communication changed from a conversation to my reacting with *cavemanesque* grunts.

I asked myself: "What just happened here?" I was experiencing shame and I felt hurt, because I'd *heard* Holly label me as defective. In fact, I really knew she was kidding. But I was unconsciously getting a sense of personal value from my performance as a painter. Holly's joke had drawn attention to my imperfection, so I reacted. I had instantly thrown up walls to protect myself from Holly. And I'd also decided that to protect myself from further indictments, I would not do any more painting.

Please notice this: On a conscious level I would never get my sense of adequacy or value from painting. But then again, that is the struggle to grow in faith—to be more and more conscious of the fact that I must draw my sense of value and acceptance from God, and how He sees me, and what He has done for me in Christ. When I do that I am free to respond, not be caught in the trap of reacting. In my marriage, I don't have to push Holly away. If I am hurt I can say, "When you said that, I felt hurt." This gives her the chance to say she is sorry or to ask me to explain my feelings and my reaction.

This is communication that builds intimacy.

I would not want to convey that my marriage to Holly has been without problems. It has been a lot of work. I have not been able to meet all of her needs, and she has not been able to meet all of mine. There are times when I treat her as my false god—that is, I sometimes get my sense of value and acceptance from how she looks, what she thinks, or how she performs. And when I do, my love and acceptance of her, my serving and equipping, turns into fixing and controlling.

But it is not Holly's job to be my source. She is a resource, a gift to me from my true Source. Her job is to be a "suitable helper." In fact, she has been much more to me than that. She has used her "femaleness" to help me become the man God wants me to be. Her empathy and sensitivity have enabled her to support me through times of pain for which I had no words. She has taught me about listening to God. I have learned from her about enjoying our children. And the joy of living with an artist has provided this meat-and-potatoes-guy with awareness of a whole new world of sights, sounds, and feelings to appreciate.

I thank God for her.

DISCUSSION QUESTIONS

1. *How does seeing God as our Source free us from undue expectations from our spouse?*

2. *Why is it necessary when one marries to truly leave one's family and cleave to one's spouse?*

3. *What are the dangers of codependency in a relationship?*

4. *Describe how healthy communication is more than just talking more.*

5. *Give examples of saying what you mean to say without controlling someone.*

14. The Grace-Full Parent

The dog-training video I mentioned in chapter 10 starts out this way: A hunter is screaming bribes and threats as he chases his dog through a field toward the camera. As the two pass out of sight, the narrator walks into the picture. "This is an example of what you don't want to happen with your dog," he laughs. Then he gets serious and continues, "The problems that arise in training a dog are almost always with the *humans*. The dog is rarely the problem."

In my experience as a family counselor, I have come to believe that the problems that arise in parenting a child are most often with the *parents*. The child is rarely the problem. Let me illustrate:

Several years ago a young couple came in for counseling concerning domestic violence on the part of the husband. They arrived at the office fifteen minutes late and in the midst of an argument. On top of that, they brought their two-year-old daughter into the room and the wife announced apologetically, "We couldn't find a sitter. We hope it's okay that we brought her. We could leave if you'd like."

I reassured them that it was fine this time and we began the session. As time went on, I noticed two things. First, the little girl didn't seem to be able to say very many words, the cause of which became apparent because her parents did all of her talking for her. Second, it also became apparent that I was more comfortable that their little girl was in the session than they were. As far as I was concerned, she was mostly acting like a normal, curious, active two-year-old. While she did seem a little out of control at times—which made it hard for us to talk—both parents seemed easily irritated at almost everything she did. They spent most of the session trying to control her behavior.

Here is how the session went:

Amy, the little girl, comes over beside me. I smile and tell her I'm happy to meet her. The dad looks irritated. Mom notices the dad's nonverbal signals and asks the daughter to come and sit by her. The daughter blurts "No!" and starts crying. (After all, she had just made a new friend.) The mom says, "I'll give you a red gumball if you stop crying and come over here by me." The girl stops crying and goes to her mom.

Three minutes later, Amy tries to get the mom's wallet out of her purse. The mom says, "No." The daughter starts crying. The dad looks irritated (progressively irritated, with each event). The mom notices, and tells Amy to stop crying. She cries harder. Mom says, "I'll give you a red gumball if you stop." The girl stops and receives a gumball.

Then she slaps the mom on the shoulder. "If you do that again you're getting spanked," hisses the mom. Amy hits her again. The dad quickly says, "I'll hold her," and picks her up. "If you calm down I'll give you a gumball," he says. Amy calms down . . . *ad nauseam.*

Finally I said, "Would you folks mind if I tried something?" Both indicated their permission.

I said, "Amy, could you come here please?" She came over by me.

Then I said, "Do you remember the friendly lady (the receptionist) you met when you first got here?"

"Uh-huh."

"Well," I continued, "you can choose to stop hitting and crying, and sit with your mom or dad. If you do, you can stay in here with us. Or you can choose to keep crying and running around. If you choose that, you will spend the rest of the time out with the lady, so your mommy and daddy and I can finish our talk. It's up to you. What is your choice?"

At that point she stopped crying and whining, hopped up on her dad's lap and started playing with one of the toys they had brought for her.

Both parents gasped simultaneously. "I don't believe it," said Amy's mom, who had worn herself out with efforts to control her child.

What happened here? There are several things we can learn from the interaction between Amy and her parents. First, these parents were bribing their daughter with sugar to get her to calm down. Calming a child with sugar is a contradiction, physiologically doomed to fail. Second, they were teaching her that acting out of control was a way to get a gumball. True, they thought they were rewarding her for cooperating. But fussing first, *then* cooperating is what did the trick. Third, instead of it being Amy's responsibility to control her behavior, it had become her parents'. Amy was not learning to control herself. But like laboratory rats, she had taught them how and when to give her gumballs.

Fourth, and most sad, Amy was learning that her behavior had a lot of power to control how her parents were feeling. When this happens, parents no longer discipline in the child's best interest. They control in order to fix the child, so that when the child is fixed they feel good about themselves. We are back to seeing the curse in action.

I also want you to see some things about my interaction with

Amy. First, I used the control I had—over the environment, not Amy—to influence her choice. Rather than trying to control her behavior, I used my authority to empower her to control her own behavior. Second, this had the effect of making her poor choices her problem instead of her parents' problem (or mine). Third, I am better able to maintain peace of mind when Amy's, or my own children's behavior, is their problem and not mine. With Amy's parents, they could only stay calm if Amy complied with their control. This gave Amy's behavior a lot of power over her parents' state of mind. And lastly, two-year-olds are capable of making wise choices and controlling themselves—when given the opportunity.

CONTROL, INFLUENCE, AND EMPOWERMENT

Earlier I advanced the opinion that the problems that arise in parenting a child are most often problems with the parents. By that I do not mean that parents are *responsible* for the choices of their children: Children are responsible for their own choices. The goal of parenting is to help children be responsible for their own choices, just as parents are to be responsible for their choices.

The problem is that as a parent and an adult, I have a lot of power and authority—physically, emotionally, mentally, and spiritually. Because I have the power to do so, I can mistakenly think I also have the *obligation* to control many things. And it is true that learning to control what I can and should control will have a profound and positive influence on the lives of my children and wife—and in every other relationship, for that matter.

I cannot make my children be honest, for instance. But I can influence them toward honesty by controlling whether I tell the truth. I cannot make them trust me, but I can control whether I mean what I say. I cannot make them trust in Jesus, but I can influence them toward faith by fighting to trust in Jesus as they watch how I live. I cannot make my kids obey. But I can control my responses to their disobedience—that is, I can respect their choices and provide wise consequences for their actions, so they can learn just as much about wisdom from disobeying as from obeying. And I can respond in ways that create an environment in which their poor choices are their problem. As I do these things they will be influenced and empowered to make wise choices.

So you see, I do have a lot of control. I'm sure that by now you also see this: I do not believe I am to control the behavior of my children. They must be learning to control themselves; I am to use my power to empower them to do so.

There is a tremendous difference in what results when you attempt to control your children's behavior, and when you empower them to control their own. The first path leads to disempowerment. The second leads to empowerment. The first to external compliance, the second to wise decision-making. The first to living out of fear, the second to living out of fullness.

COMPLIANCE VS. OBEDIENCE

It is utterly evident from Scriptures like 1 Samuel 16:6, 7 and Matthew 23:25 that God cares about hearts. As Christian parents, we should too.

A few years back a church invited me to lead a weekend workshop on some of the concepts presented in this book. A woman raised her hand and asked, "Do you think parents should make their children go to church?"

I replied, "If your kids go to church because you make them, don't call that spiritual health on the part of your kids."

"But don't you think you should still make them go?" she pressed. It was obvious at that point that this is what she thought, and she would have felt better if I had thought so too.

"It's okay to have a family rule about going to church and to insist that your children go. Just don't be naïve about it. If they go because they're forced, don't mistake that for their caring about God," I answered.

She was very frustrated.

Whether your children go to church or should be made to go to church is not my point in telling this story. I tell it because I want you to consider the *whys* of behavior at least as much as the *whats*. *Compliance* with external pressure means a child has been squeezed into a mold; he is being conformed from the outside/in. *Obedience* is about learning to live consistent on the outside with what God is doing on the inside.

THE PURPOSE OF CONSEQUENCES

Many parents don't understand the purpose of consequences. Here are some *do's* and *don'ts*:

Do not give children consequences for the purpose of punishing them for wrong behavior. I have noticed that people who grow up in families or churches with "punishing mindsets" have difficulty experiencing forgiveness as a gift. They seem to have a need to earn forgiveness by paying for or making up for what they did. Jesus Christ has already taken the punishment for all of our wrong behavior.

Do not give consequences in order to threaten children into acting the way you want them to. People who do this are trying to control their children's behavior by simply teaching them to act in ways that avoid pain. At best, this promotes compliance and people-pleasing, not wise decision-making. Children who learn to avoid pain at all costs become adults who are afraid to try new things. Some adults sacrifice their integrity and people-please a boss they can't stand in order to keep a job they hate. When do you think they learned this behavior? And what happens when these children are no longer in an environment that molds them in a positive direction? They may learn in their new environment that using drugs, being

183

sexually active—or simply choosing to follow the crowd—are ways to avoid pain.

Do give your children consequences in order to teach about behavior. As long as you are going to do a lot of work in being a parent (and you are), *do the right work.* You can spend your energy trying to keep track of, control, and fix your children through bribes, threats, and sermons. Or you can spend your energy discovering and implementing consequences from which your children can learn about the wisdom of their choices and their ability to make good ones. Children can learn as much from disobeying and receiving wise consequences as they can from obeying.

Do allow your children to experience the natural consequences of their behavior. I am not suggesting that you let your three-year-old play in the street to learn about what happens when he does that. You're going to have to use your head on this one.

Consider the following example. Ten years ago I was on an errand with Kara, who was then seven years old, and Jesi, who was three. I noticed in the rearview mirror that Kara was tormenting Jesi in a variety of big-sister ways. Suddenly, Jesi clobbered her with a left upper-cut.

"Daddy, Jesi hit me," came Kara's lament.

"Think about what just happened," I answered. Kara thought about it for all of twenty seconds. Then, in the mirror, I noticed that her tormenting began anew.

POW! Jesi let her have it again.

"Jesi hit me again," Kara cried.

"Kara, I know that you are capable of figuring out how not to get slugged," I answered. I watched in the mirror as Kara thought about it. And then, *click* I saw the light go on. The tormenting stopped.

Yes, Kara was acting inappropriately. But through that interaction I sent Kara the message that she was capable of thinking and of making wise choices. Helping a child to make these wise connections is, perhaps, the most significant part of the disciplining process. I also allowed Kara's behavior and its consequences to remain her problem. My own dad, like many others, would have just stopped the car and spanked everyone he could reach. Our behavior would have become his to control, instead of a chance for us to learn.

True, the disciplining job was not over when Kara learned that she was capable of making a better choice. I was also presented with an opportunity to teach Jesi that she can make a different choice than hitting. I said, "Jesi, it's not okay for you to hit Kara. If you feel sad or angry about what she is doing, you are capable of saying it in words without hitting." Kara's consequence was clear, if she continued her tormenting behavior. Jesi's was not so clear to her, and if she continued to hit I would then have to find a way to make her hitting *her problem* instead of Kara's or mine. This is the work of parenting.

YOU MUST FOLLOW THROUGH

Consequences and follow-through are of utmost importance. If you do not or cannot follow through to enforce what you ask of your child, don't ask it. If your daughter is hitting her sister, you might say, "Stop hitting your sister." If she continues hitting, you can continue to say, "Stop hitting"—and you may throw in a sermon about hitting, but if nothing else happens to transfer responsibility for her behavior from you to her, she may learn several things you don't want her to learn.

First, she learns that "stop hitting" really means, "I don't like you to hit, but it's okay to keep hitting." She's also learning to communicate what she is feeling by hitting instead of with words. And she's learning that if she can put up with a little lecturing she can continue to hurt people.

Say this instead: "You can choose to stop hitting, and continue to stay here and play. Or you can choose to keep hitting." Because face it, really she could. "But if you do, you will have to go into your room . . ." (or another consequence you are capable of devising) ". . . until you can come back and choose not to be hurtful. What is your choice?" *Then you need to follow through.*

If you say, "You can go out after your room is clean"—you need to follow through. If you say, "Sure you can spend your money on CDs, but you won't have any for those shoes you wanted"—don't supply money when you hear a sob story down the road. Don't say, "What's wrong with you? I told you to save your money!" Instead, you can say, "I know that you're capable of figuring out how to have money the next time you want new shoes."

It is work to create and follow through with consequences, but not as much as thinking and acting like it's your job to control the actions of your children. Pick your work.

LEARN TO ASK YOURSELF THE *INSIDE* QUESTIONS

Earlier, we saw that human beings have basic inner needs that fit into three categories: We need to know that we are loved and accepted without strings; that we are valuable, important, and capable; and that we are not alone to face life. Here I want to challenge you to think of behavior in terms of its relationship to the child's needs. In other words, when your child is disobeying, acting hurtful to others, or misbehaving in other ways, begin to ask yourself the question, "Which need are they trying to meet with this behavior?"

By asking yourself this important question, you are becoming a parent to your child's inner needs, not just a trainer and controller of outward behaviors. You can use even their inappropriate behavior as an opportunity to respond to their needs. This may eliminate the reason for the child's inappropriate actions. You may also realize that their behavior is simply a crooked way to ask for a need to be filled. For instance, clinging may be a crooked way to say, "I need love, I feel unimportant, I am lonely."

Now you have an opportunity to teach them to ask for things straight. For instance, when one child hits another, it may be a crooked way of saying, "I don't like how I'm being treated. I feel like I don't matter." In this case, that child needs to learn to say that in words. The other child needs to be given information about how their behavior affects people. Both are capable of making better choices.

Or let's say that your child is hounding you to play, and no matter how many times you tell them to stop it, they just continue. You may find that they will choose to stop acting that way if you say, "If you want attention, you can ask for it in words." (This works for children of all ages and spouses as well.) If they ask, you can give it to them, or you can say, "I will spend time with you in thirty minutes. First, I need to finish what I'm doing." Then you must follow through.

When your child yells at you, is it because they are rebelling against authority? Do you think they need to show more respect for their parents? Or is it that they feel unimportant, or that no one is listening, and so they choose to get loud in order to be heard? Ask the inner question, and you may learn something about your child that surprises you.

When a teenager becomes involved in premarital sex, is it just because of raging hormones? Is it simply a matter of ignoring the rules? Or could it be an attempt to feel loved and accepted, important, or not alone? I think so. I believe it is easier for teenagers to wait for sex until they are married when they sense their inner needs for acceptance, love, and companionship are being met at home in healthy ways. They need to be reminded that they are unconditionally loved.

PARENTING OUT OF FULLNESS

Learning to ask the above kinds of questions will set you free to parent for the right reasons. In other words, *children's choices are their responsibility, and result from how they decide to meet their own needs.* Once you understand this, you can learn to stop interpreting their choices as statements about you. When your kids act weird in front of the in-laws, it is about their choices, not about your value as a person. Grace-full in-laws will already know that. You need to know that too. Otherwise, you will parent to fix your kids, so that when they are fixed, you are fixed. You will parent to control, not to serve. How things look and what people think will become more important than what is real.

Your children should not have to act appropriately so that you can feel like a valuable person. It is not their job to validate you or erase past relationship indictments against you with their performance. In a healthy Christian family *children are not there for the adults, adults are there to be resources for their children.*

Your first responsibility as a parent is to take care of yourself. A cared-for parent is a more adequate resource to his/her family members, and is less likely to attempt to control others in order to feel worthwhile as a result of their performance.

EVERYONE IS RESPONSIBLE FOR HIS/HER OWN BEHAVIOR . . .

If your child reports that a sibling or classmate has treated him/her cruelly, don't ask, "Well, what did you do to deserve it?" No one ever deserves to be mistreated—not children or adults. This response indicates that under certain conditions it is okay to treat someone in a cruel way. Think: Do you really want your child to think this?

The other person acted cruelly because they chose to do so. No one *made* them do anything. Your child is as powerless to make them act cruelly as he/she is to make them act kindly. If your child is doing something inappropriate, to which the other person is responding unkindly, you can help your child find a different way to act. We must teach our children to be responsible for their own behavior, not for the behavior of others.

. . .INCLUDING PARENTS

Taking responsibility for behavior applies to parents as well. Don't blame your children for your choices. Don't say, "If you would listen—or behave—I wouldn't have to yell." Your children are not responsible for your yelling. You are. *You don't have to yell. You are capable of finding other ways to deal with your frustration.* The person who needs to change so you can stop yelling is *you*. This also applies to hitting, walking out, swearing, having headaches or upset stomachs, and pouting.

It is also our responsibility to make sure standards, requests, and consequences are clearly communicated. For example, if you say you are going to the State Fair on Saturday, you should go because you said you would. It is not okay to decide on Saturday that the family will stay home because someone didn't clean his room on Friday.

Family members need to receive what was promised because it was promised, not because they earn it or deserve it. Don't change your commitment based on your children's behavior. At that point you are bailing-out on going where you promised because of your decision to punish, not because of their behavior. You chose to break a promise. Instead, think of a different consequence related to a messy room or whatever else is the problem. It would be fine in the first place to have said, "After your rooms are clean on Saturday, we'll go to the Fair." Then their choice not to clean their rooms is also their vote to stay home.

KIDS NEED TO LEARN TO DO THEIR OWN WORK

Children are famous for trying to get adults to do work they can do themselves. Sometimes this is because they don't feel powerful enough or capable of doing it.

Instead of *triangling* (becoming the third person in a relationship between two people), empower your children to do their own relationship work.

One day, Callie came to me and said, "Erin is using my markers."

This is a code that means "I don't like this and I want you to fix it."

I said, "Did you give her permission?"

"No," Callie answered.

"Have you talked to her about it?" I asked.

"No."

"I think you should try talking to her. Go ahead, you're capable," I encouraged.

Off she marched.

"Erin," I overheard Callie say, "I don't like that you are using my markers without asking. I want them back."

"Okay," Erin said. Then she said, "Callie, can I *borrow* your markers?"

"Okay," chirped Callie.

I could not believe my ears. Not only had Callie done her own work, but it worked for her! And with so little effort on my part. It was not that Callie was selfish and did not want to share. It was that she felt discounted because she was not asked first.

As every parent knows, it will not always work like this. Sometimes the person using the markers will say, "Nuts to you" or "So?" At that point the owner of the markers needs to be empowered and encouraged. In that case I might go with her and stand next to her as she does the work. If the other person refuses or is stubborn, I might say, "I want you to listen to your sister and make a respectful choice." If she still refuses, I would say, "You can choose to . . . or you can choose . . . What is your choice?"

It takes a lot of work *not* to get in there and try to control how everyone feels and acts. But with practice, you'll get the hang of it.

AN ACCURATE PICTURE OF JESUS

When Erin was about two years old, she proudly presented me with this picture:

I noticed that the person in the picture was bald and that the name on the bottom started with the letters J and E. I wasn't paying careful attention and I incorrectly assumed she had drawn a picture of me. (I couldn't figure out why I had three eyes, though. But then I realized that when you are two years old and looking up at a bald guy, his nose looks like it is between his eyes.)

Then I looked again at the name below. *Jesus.* I lost my breath. I felt like I had been hit in the stomach. This is what Jesus looked like to Erin: like me. It made me wonder if I looked like Him.

No, I am not to take the place of God in my children's lives. But, like Jesus, I am to present to my family the grace of God. As a parent, am I sending out verbal and nonverbal messages—"Not good enough"; "Something's wrong with you"; "Try harder"—or do I mirror Jesus, whose stance toward them is one of unconditional love, who reminds them of their profound worth, and who offers the support they need in order to live?

God loves me with a love that went all the way to the cross. I think it's good to think about that every so often.

CONCLUSION

I have offered the principles in this book not as standards to measure up to, but rather as new ways to think about God, His grace, and how it can become real and life-changing for you and your family. If you are a believer, your value and identity is settled because of Jesus. It is not up to your family members to validate you with their performance. You are free to let go of controlling; you can learn what it means to serve without becoming everyone's slave. You can learn more and more to act toward others out of a new spiritual fullness.

With God's grace, you can become a more effective, more grace-full husband, wife, parent. As these truths sink deep into your heart, yours will be more and more a family where grace is in place.

DISCUSSION QUESTIONS

1. *Read the story of a couple who came to their counseling session with their two-year-old. How does this show that the problems that arise in parenting a child are most often with the parents?*

2. *Which is more important: to control your children, or to teach them to control themselves? Explain.*

3. *Describe the difference between compliance and obedience.*

4. *How does a child's behavior sometimes relate to his basic inner needs?*

5. *Give examples of the difference between parenting in the best interests of the child and parenting to look good to others or to "fix" your own problems.*